Alfred

The Autobiography of a Quaker Nationalist

IRISH NARRATIVES

IRISH NARRATIVES

Series edited by David Fitzpatrick

Personal narratives of past lives are essential for understanding any field of history. They provide unrivalled insight into the day-to-day consequences of political, social, economic or cultural relationships. Memoirs, diaries and personal letters, whether by public figures or obscure witnesses of historical events, will often captivate the general reader as well as engrossing the specialist. Yet the vast majority of such narratives are preserved only among the manuscripts or rarities in libraries and archives scattered over the globe. The aim of this series of brief yet scholarly editions is to make available a wide range of narratives concerning Ireland and the Irish over the last four centuries. All documents, or sets of documents, are edited and introduced by specialist scholars, who guide the reader through the world in which the text was created. The chosen texts are faithfully transcribed, the biographical and local background explored, and the documents set in historical context. This series will prove invaluable for university and school teachers, providing superb material for essays and textual analysis in class. Above all, it offers a novel opportunity for readers interested in Irish history to discover fresh and exciting sources of personal testimony.

Other titles in the series:

Andrew Bryson's Ordeal: An Epilogue to the 1798 Rebellion, edited by Michael Durey
Henry Stratford Persse's Letters from Galway to America, 1821–1832, edited by James L. Pethica and James C. Roy
A Redemptorist Missionary in Ireland, 1851–1854: Memoirs by Joseph Prost, translated and edited by Emmet Larkin and Herman Freudenberger
Frank Henderson's Easter Rising, edited by Michael Hopkinson
A Patriot Priest: The Life of Father James Coigly, 1761–1798, edited by Dáire Keogh
'My Darling Danny': Letters from Mary O'Connell to her son Daniel, 1830–1832, edited by Erin I. Bishop
The Rebel in his Family: Selected Papers of William Smith O'Brien, edited by Richard and Marianne Davis
The Reynolds Letters: An Irish Emigrant Family in Late Victorian Manchester, edited by Lawrence W. McBride
A Policeman's Ireland: Recollections of Samuel Waters, RIC, edited by Stephen Ball
'The Misfit Soldier': Edward Casey's War Story, 1914–1918, edited by Joanna Bourke

Forthcoming titles:

Pádraig Ó Fathaigh's War of Independence: Recollections of a Galway Gaelic Leaguer, edited by Timothy G. McMahon

David Fitzpatrick teaches history at Trinity College, Dublin. His books include *Politics and Irish Life, 1913–1921* (1977, reissued 1998) and *Oceans of Consolation: Personal Accounts of Irish Migration to Australia* (1995).

Alfred Webb
The Autobiography of a Quaker Nationalist

Edited by
Marie-Louise Legg

CORK UNIVERSITY PRESS

First published in 1999 by
Cork University Press
Cork
Ireland

© Cork University Press 1999

British Library Cataloguing in Publication Data
A CIP catalogue record for this book is available from the British Library.

ISBN 1 85918 202 X

Typesetting by Red Barn Publishing, Skeagh, Skibbereen

Printed in Ireland by ColourBooks, Baldoyle, Co. Dublin

Contents

Acknowledgements

When I was working on the nineteenth-century Irish press, Roy Foster suggested that I should read Alfred Webb's autobiography. As ever, I am deeply grateful to him for this, and for his encouragement in this project. I am particularly indebted to Mary Shackleton, the Curator of the Friends' Historical Library and to her assistants for their help in transcribing the text. Pamela Bradley allowed me to consult her valuable Biographical Index to Webb's text which helped me to unravel the complex relationships of the many Quaker families in his circle, and Richard Harrison advised me on general Quaker questions. Mary Clark at the Dublin Corporation Archives and Gerry Daly at the Port and Docks Board gave answers to specific queries, and librarians at Trinity College, Dublin, the National Library of Ireland, the Royal Irish Academy, and the Oriental and India Office Library, London have been, as ever, very supportive.

Introduction

Alfred Webb was one of numerous Protestants who worked for the advancement of Irish nationalism. Now almost forgotten, he could never be described as a major public figure, but he was an indispensable supporter of the movement for Home Rule, both as a key administrator and as a pillar of moral probity. Born into a Quaker family, he acknowledges in his autobiography that it was the memory of the disabilities suffered by religious dissenters that gave him, and many Quakers like him, a special concern for the wrongs done to Irish Catholics. Webb was drawn into the movement for Home Rule in the mid-1860s and served as secretary or treasurer of the organisations conducting successive campaigns: the Home Government Association, the Home Rule League, the National League, the Irish Parliamentary Party and the United Irish League. Despite disappointments with their leaders and despair at those who were diverted from the main goal, his patient and conscientious work was exceptionally valuable. But if he is now largely forgotten in Ireland, Webb's place in the advancement of nationalism is still remembered in India, where his name was associated with those of Annie Besant and Sir William Wedderburn during the fiftieth anniversary celebrations of Indian independence.[1]

Nineteenth-century Quaker society was exceptionally close-knit. Although marrying outside the Society of Friends was becoming more usual, families tended to confine socialising to within the circle of its meetings. Webb's grandfather, James Webb, was a weaver from Loughgall, County Armagh. He married Deborah Sparrow from Forrest, County Wexford. James Webb came to Dublin and founded a drapery business, and their son Richard Davis Webb was born there in 1805. He attended the Quaker school in Ballitore where Edmund Burke had been educated in the 1740s, and as a young man he went to France, where he met Lafayette.[2]

Richard Webb was apprenticed to a Dublin Quaker printer and later founded a bookshop and printing business in South William Street. In 1832 he married Hannah Waring from Waterford. They moved to 160

Great Brunswick Street, now Pearse Street, where he went into partnership with Robert Chapman. Alfred, their first child, was born there a year later on 10 June 1834. There were eventually three more children, Richard, Deborah and Anne. Richard Davis Webb was commercially successful, but he had wider interests both national and international. Like many Quakers, he was involved in the Hibernian Temperance Society and used his business to advance the cause, printing tracts, pamphlets, textbooks and newspapers. Both Richard Davis and Hannah Webb were active in the anti-slavery movement and worked with successive Dublin anti-slavery societies. Through the anti-slavery movement, the Webbs met the American abolitionist, William Lloyd Garrison, with whom they shared opinions on temperance and women's suffrage, and they visited him in Boston. When Frederick Douglass, the American freed slave, came to Dublin in 1845, Webb published his biography and arranged meetings for him to address. Together with other Quakers, the elder Webb campaigned against British imperial policy during the opium wars and against the rule of the East India Company.[3]

Irish Quakers have been described as neither 'established Protestants nor Catholics', and this sense of 'apartness' informed their social and political attitudes. R. D. Webb was deeply concerned about the 'distorting glasses of sectarian prejudice'.[4] He had instinctively supported Repeal, but feared that Daniel O'Connell's creation of a Roman Catholic mass party would fuel sectarian division. Thus he dissented from O'Connell's monster meetings, where the ignorant and bigoted might be urged to insurrection.[5] Alfred Webb had a memory of being taken to see O'Connell in Richmond Bridewell in 1844. As pacifists, Richard Davis Webb and a group of his friends, known as 'the Faction', advanced their progressive views at public meetings. The elder Webb believed that Irish Quakers were almost all Tories. The Society of Friends was split between those who adhered closely to the literal word of the Bible and those who embraced wider views. Like his father, Alfred Webb chafed against their innate conservatism and embraced the radical wing. Both father and son resigned from the Society. Alfred

Webb told members of the Dublin Monthly Meeting in 1858 that he disagreed with their opinions, and that in order to act consistently he must withdraw.[6]

Friends provided disinterested, compassionate and effective relief during the Famine, free in the main from the stain of proselytism. Richard Davis Webb and Archbishop Whately gave relief to those who had been persecuted for having converted in order to receive food. Webb became an honorary inspector for the Quaker Relief Committee. In 1847 Alfred Webb, then aged thirteen, had urged the Society of Friends to start a Famine Relief Fund. In later life he said that the Famine marked a division between the world of Maria Edgeworth, Charles Lever and William Carleton, and the Ireland of 1848, Fenianism and the Land League. The experience had humiliated Ireland, which had been 'peeped and botanized upon by persons from all parts of the world'.[7]

Alfred Webb's parents tried to educate their children in an atmosphere free of sectarian bias, and Webb was first taught at home by private tutors. He was then sent to Dr Hodgson's High School in Manchester. Hodgson was a Unitarian who held advanced theories on education.[8] In 1853 Webb went to Australia for his health. He tried his hand at gold-digging, but without success, and spent most of his time there working on road construction. In Australia he saw the Aborigines' loss of land and its consequences, and felt deep sympathy for their plight.[9] On his return to Dublin in 1855, he began work in the family business, and in 1861 he married his cousin Elizabeth Shackleton of Ballitore.[10] From the mid-1850s he deepened his involvement in every radical movement.

The autobiography which Webb wrote at the end of his life is not just the story of his own life, it is also an important record of Dublin in the middle of the nineteenth century. Great Brunswick Street was part of the city's developing commercial centre. The Webb printing business and home was set between two coal merchants and surrounded by other trades: billiard-table makers, solicitors, oboe teachers and statuary and ornament manufacturers.[11] There was only one short railway line to Kingstown, and people still travelled in sedan chairs over streets which were unpaved and reduced to mud in the winter. There was no main drainage, and the poor drew water from street fountains. The printing shop was lit by tallow candles.[12] Alfred Webb's description of his parents' involvement in the business and his own early introduction to setting type demonstrates how close-knit the family was both in ideals and action. With his parents, he threw himself into the anti-slavery movement, urging that 'this subject will be more thought upon in this colony'.[13] Quakers were divided between supporters of the doctrine of non-resistance who associated women's rights with anti-slavery, and those who thought them irrelevant to the issue. This tension between the quietist approach and militant action was faced by Alfred Webb in the 1880s when he became secretary of the National League.

Webb campaigned for the disestablishment of the Church of Ireland. He was a member of the committee of the Dublin branch of the National Association for the Repeal of the Contagious Diseases Act.[14] He supported women's suffrage, on the slightly unusual grounds that women, being the weaker sex, needed equal legal rights.[15] He campaigned for Sunday closing, for a clean water supply for Dublin, and for the opening of St Stephen's Green to the public.[16] He was a town councillor for the Inns Quay ward in Dublin and served on the Ports and Harbour Board. Influenced as he was by his father's concern with human rights and relationships, Alfred Webb moved on to the issues central to Ireland's future, Home Rule and the reform of land tenure.

Webb rejected the idea that a people should be satisfied with just the provision of food, clothing and housing: 'There must be some national life and feeling . . . all history bears a record to it.'[17] He urged the study of Ireland's past, believing that its reconstruction was 'one of the most difficult . . . tasks any people could undertake'.[18] Like W. E. H. Lecky, Webb was deeply critical of the treatment of Ireland in the English press, which used 'scornful, contemptuous language' and had 'the effect of creating a feeling of repulsion towards England in the minds of a large portion of the Irish people'.[19] Reversing the ideal of Repeal, he suggested that Irish parliaments should be held in England, that Irish regiments should wear distinctive dress, and that there should be an Irish flag.[20]

Two events brought Alfred Webb into nationalist politics. The first occurred in 1865 when his father was called on to serve as a juror in the Fenian trials. Richard Davis Webb was ill and asked his son to go to Green Street courthouse to present a certificate of his incapacity. Webb's sense of injustice was roused at the sight of the prisoners, Thomas Clarke Luby, Jeremiah O'Donovan Rossa and John O'Leary, in the dock where Emmet had been sentenced to death in 1803. As he wrote later, this was a moment 'like Paul on his road to Damascus'[21]. In a letter to the *Manchester Examiner* he rejected the accusation that journalists on the *Irish People* had been engaged in a mass conspiracy. The Fenian movement was, he said, 'an expression of that longing after nationality — after some country to love, and some way of showing love for it — which is one of the strongest feelings of our nation'.[22] Webb became drawn into the movement to support the prisoners' families and into the Amnesty campaign. The second occasion on which his eyes were opened was on a visit to Cork immediately after the 1867 rising. Mass arrests were made and trials held by Special Commission. His relatives told him that Cork prison was full of Fenians.[23]

In the Dublin court Webb had heard Isaac Butt speaking in Luby's defence. Webb shared Butt's understanding of the need for what Joseph Spence has called an 'ecumenical Irishness', believing that it was possible for both Catholics and Protestants to support justice for Ireland.[24] Webb joined Butt's Home Government Association and was soon acting as an honorary secretary. Butt used the Association to put forward a federal programme for Ireland with a parliament in Dublin. It did not advocate Repeal, and Repeal was the touchstone for the Catholic liberals whose backing the Association badly needed. The Home Government Association never gained wide support outside Dublin because its reputation as an essentially conservative body deterred both liberals and Catholics.[25] Webb recognised this himself: 'The smallness of the support we are receiving is very discouraging,' he wrote to W. J. O'Neill

Daunt in 1871.[26] When the Home Rule League was founded in 1873, Webb became its treasurer. The League brought in all those who had kept away from the Home Government Association: priests, advanced nationalists and liberals. It seemed a hopeful time: Mitchell Henry told Webb that Home Rule would be carried in three years.[27]

But Webb became increasingly disillusioned with Butt's leadership and the movement's failure to unite the whole nation behind the cause. Calling it a 'moribund agitation', he resigned his office. His moderate friends congratulated him on withdrawing from the campaign, but he knew that it was only a matter of time before he again became involved. In October 1879 the Irish National Land League was formed. Webb never joined the Land League, probably because of its links with Fenianism and the Irish Republican Brotherhood; but his sympathy with its aims was such that he travelled all over Ireland speaking on its behalf. When the political organisation of the Irish Parliamentary Party, the National League, replaced the Land League in 1882, Webb became its acting treasurer. In this capacity he was responsible for the delicate task of distributing funds to members of the Irish Parliamentary Party, to the branches of the League, to lawyers defending Irish MPs and journalists, and to funds supporting evicted tenants. It was a job requiring the utmost patience and tact, and one which frequently challenged his innate sense of probity. He risked imprisonment by helping to conceal the funds of the Land League, and he put his livelihood in danger by concealing the National League's papers and by printing pamphlets for the Ladies' Land League. He condemned intimidation in the League's name. He resisted the payment of grants to branches which had committed such offences, and made no secret of his dislike for the tone and cartoons of *United Ireland*. It was intimidation and violence that horrified Webb, not breaking the law. He recalled his own father's refusal, as a Dissenter, to pay tithes to the Established Church, and how his furniture had been seized and sold. If Irishmen had not broken the law in the past, they would have been swept away.[28] Underlying his unhappiness was his belief that a 'great national movement' could not be run with 'the looseness of organisation or toleration of the language' of the Land

League. Increasingly he was uneasy with Parnell's autocratic mode of leadership and made it known that he would prefer to be unobtrusively replaced as treasurer, as he might feel obliged to make a public protest.[29]

The Curtin affair in 1885 epitomised Webb's increasing isolation from the programme and activities of the League, and his treatment at the hands of Parnell.[30] John O'Connell Curtin, a Kerry farmer, was shot dead in November 1885 by moonlighters searching for arms. One man was killed by Curtin, and the others were later arrested. The Curtin family gave evidence at their trial, as a result of which the family was boycotted and attacked and had to have police protection. Following the trial, Alfred Webb travelled to Kerry to investigate the incident and its aftermath. Here he saw the family being hooted when they attended mass. When Webb addressed the crowd outside the church, women dragged the pew where he had sat with the family into the churchyard and smashed it. Stones were thrown, and the police had to disperse the crowd.[31] The murder of John Curtin was denounced in the national press in England and Ireland, and the London *Times* used the incident to further the association between Parnellism and crime. Webb was appalled by his experience in Kerry, and felt that it was the duty of all nationalists to stand by the family and to repudiate the 'shameful and horrible calumnies afloat in Dublin'.[32] He wrote an article for the *Freeman's Journal*, but the newspaper asked him to delay it, and Parnell stopped its publication. When Webb was advised to desist by men he considered his friends, he was deeply depressed and felt that they had been disingenuous about the activities of the League branches.

Webb entered parliament unopposed, after a by-election in February 1890. During his five years as member for West Waterford he spoke mainly on Irish affairs and particularly on shipping and navigation. But his greatest achievement as an Irish MP was to be invited to preside at the Tenth Indian National Congress in Madras in 1894. Irish nationalists had for some time recognised that India and Ireland had the goals of self-government and land reform in common. John Stuart Mill had found parallels between Irish and Indian land tenure problems.[33] Frank Hugh O'Donnell claimed that he had been approached by Indian nationalists who offered to support Irish nationalism if in return Ireland would elect Indian members to speak for India at Westminster.[34] Webb told John Dillon that Gopal Gokhale, an Indian law professor, had a more accurate knowledge of Irish history and politics than many members of the Irish Party.[35] The Parsee nationalist Dadabhai Naoroji[36] had formulated the 'drain' theory: that India had been depleted of its wealth by the British. He had a longstanding interest in Ireland and thought that 'it was exceedingly desirable that the lesson of Ireland should be taken for India', although he did not believe that the objectives of the two countries were identical.[37] Michael Davitt invited Naoroji to stand for a constituency in the west of Ireland in the hope of giving a voice to British subjects who were ruled despotically and taxed but who had no votes. Despite encouragement from Indian nationalists, Naoroji declined Davitt's invitation on the reasonable and logical grounds that should Home Rule succeed he would not wish to find himself removed from Westminster.[38]

Webb too had seen parallels between the Irish and Indian experience of government from Westminster, and maintained that the evils of 'Castle' government in Ireland resembled those which blighted India, the latter being only 'aggravated by distance, fear and differences of race, religion and languages'. The two countries had another special relationship: Irishmen served in the army in India and drew pensions paid for by Indian taxpayers.[39]

The proposal to invite an Irishman to preside over the 1894 Congress had been made by D. E. Wacha, the president of the Bombay Presidency Association and secretary of the INC.[40] The Congress organisation in Madras wanted to have a British MP as president in 1894, underlining their commitment to parliamentary representation in India. Wacha first suggested Dr Robert Spence Watson,[41] but he then settled on Edward Blake, an Irishman who had been a liberal politician in Canada but had returned to Ireland in 1892 and become Nationalist MP for South Longford. With his experience of the federal government of Canada after the 1867 North America Act, Blake would have been an appropriate choice. However, Blake was not available, and in October the invitation was extended to Davitt himself, but Davitt declined on the ground that it would be risky for Congress to invite him.[42] Webb was then asked to take his place.

The Tenth Indian National Congress in Madras was attended by over 1,000 people. Webb's presidential address had been drafted by himself and Naoroji in London, and then revised by Wacha on Webb's arrival in Bombay, deleting many of the 'abundant references' to Ireland.[43] Despite these revisions, Webb referred to his nationality as the principal ground for his selection as president. Quoting William Lloyd Garrison, 'My country is the world; my countrymen are all mankind', his address brought together the campaigns with which he had been involved over the past forty years: anti-slavery, the fight against sectarianism, church disestablishment, and franchise reform. He spoke of the similar attitudes and language of those who ruled both India and Ireland. Many of the issues to be debated by Congress were echoed in Irish affairs: land, the freedom to carry arms, the campaign for temperance. Western civilisation owed its culture to the East, but in return it had handed back 'some of its lowest products'. As a Christian and an Irishman allied to Britain, he said he was 'almost ashamed to stand before you' and speak about the spread of drink in India and the regulation of vice.[44] His speech was praised for its simplicity and eloquence, even by the Anglo-Indian press usually hostile to Congress. Wacha wrote to Naoroji of 'your happy choice', who had won 'golden opinions all round' for his hard work, his patience, impartiality and tolerance.[45] Two years later Wacha and Gokhale visited Ireland, and Webb arranged for them to speak at the Friends' Institute.[46]

Although he wrote that he 'felt at home' in parliament at Westminster, it is clear from his correspondence that as time went on Webb felt increasingly uneasy there. He disliked the mass of his fellow parliamentarians whose drinking and behaviour were an 'utter disgrace and weakness'.[47] He found it incomprehensible that men could pass resolutions and speeches 'fatal to the movement' and with the next breath

declare their confidence that it would be successful.[48] He thought he
was not cut out to be an MP, and felt he should not have left Ireland
because he was in danger of becoming separate from its people. His
agony over the crisis brought by the O'Shea divorce and the split in the
party made what might have been a short sentence away from Ireland
now seem interminable.[49] He had a conversation with T. M. Healy in
1897 in which Healy described the corrosive effect of the split on the
Irish Party in terms of a cancerous growth.[50] Webb's suffering and its
long-term effects were so great that when, over fifteen years later, he
wrote his autobiography he described the events during the crisis in a
separate, unpaginated appendix intended only for those of his friends
and relatives who shared his views.

During and after the split Webb faced considerable difficulties in
managing the various funds headed by the National League, the
National Federation and then, in 1898, the United Irish League. Immediately after the split Webb joined with William O'Brien and John Dillon to ensure that monies sent to the National League from America
were credited to them, and not to Parnell.[51] Webb's integrity was con-
tinually challenged by issues such as whether tenants who had received
monies from the Evicted Tenants' Fund before October 1890 could
now receive monies from the United Irish League. His problems were
made worse by the disruptive behaviour of T. M. Healy.[52] In August
1895 Webb told Dillon: 'For some years my happiness or unhappiness
in life have to a not inconsiderable degree depended upon the vagaries
of Mr Healy.'[53] In August 1895, a few weeks after his re-election for
West Waterford, he resigned from the National Federation's executive
because of its failure to condemn Healy's actions. With sadness, he also
resigned from the Irish Parliamentary Party and from his seat at Westminster, to the distress of J. F. X. O'Brien and others.[54]

Webb's unhappiness was not confined to these public disagreements.
He was troubled that the intense desire for Home Rule had become dis-
sipated and replaced with complacency: 'Wherever I go I cannot but
realize how little is left of the old desires and aspirations.' Catholics who
had risen in society through the spread of nationalism had themselves

become filled with 'anti-Irish, or rather no-Irish feeling'.[55] Thirty-five years of his life had been devoted to Home Rule, he told Dillon in 1903, but 'Where now are the Protestant Home Rulers of 1870?'[56]

Webb believed that it was the duty of all men and women to take an intelligent interest and an active part in public affairs. Throughout his life he wrote letters on every topic to the press in England and Ireland, and he printed and published pamphlets written by himself and others. He was meticulous in dealing with the machinery and the politics of finance in sometimes difficult and hazardous circumstances. He possessed a capacity to sit through long meetings without complaint. When he chaired the two-day meeting of the Indian National Congress in 1894 his patience, impartiality and tolerance were praised: 'for two days the old man sat out for nearly 10 to 11 hours with an interruption of only half an hour . . . [he is] simply adored for his earnest and happy simplicity'.[57] He believed that politics were 'the most ennobling, most comprehensive spheres of human activity', but also observed that there was 'much that is ludicrous . . . sad . . . deplorable about them'.[58] Some of his colleagues, thought he was 'naïve' and emotional (at one meeting Healy reduced Webb to tears);[59] but he had internal reserves they could not perceive. Webb's weakness, and he recognised it himself, was that he was not cut out to be a national politician: 'I am too big a man to be a meer [sic] voting unit, I am too small a man to impress my views on others.'[60]

Alone of the leaders of Irish nationalism, Michael Davitt never failed Webb, and Webb admired Davitt in return. Together they had worked for Home Rule and land reform to be achieved by non-violence. Like Davitt, Webb campaigned for the Boers, against antisemitism and for temperance.[61] Davitt saw that Webb had rare qualities and recognised his role as guardian for all the movements he served. Webb never hesitated to consider whether a warning or a prudent act would be popular: he possessed 'the highest moral bravery'.[62] Towards the end of his life Alfred Webb became increasingly saddened by diversions away from the central issue of Home Rule. Home Rule had been 'snowed under by Labour, Evicted Tenants, grasslands, Town Tenants, Gaelic Revivals, Irish Manufactures, Railway, Education, Monuments and Testimonials . . . It is what I came in to fight for, and I never hear a word about it these times.'[63] He could be sardonic about sentimental Irish nationalism, suggesting that a correspondent of the Irish National Federation should be sent 'a nice Spread Eagle, Sunburst, '98, '48, '67 letter'.[64] He was lonely in the house he had built in Orwell Park: his wife Elizabeth died in 1907, and they had no children.

Alfred Webb died on 31 July 1908 in the Shetland Islands, where he had gone for a walking holiday. His obituaries spoke of the service he had given to the nationalist cause throughout his life in ways that were practical, wise and unobtrusive.[65] He was buried in the Friends' Cemetery at Temple Hill, Blackrock, County Dublin.

Editorial Note

Webb's autobiography is in two volumes of manuscript, bound in leather and covered with red cloth. They measure 5½in × 9in. Each volume contains about 280 lined folios, written on one side only, except where Webb has made subsequent interpolations on the opposite page. Webb originally asked a woman friend to write out the whole text in copperplate hand, but this took so long that it was abandoned after seventeen pages, and the rest is in Webb's own handwriting. The text, put together from diaries and notes, was written probably between October 1904 and March 1905. Originally discovered in the offices of Harveys of Waterford, which had been the offices of T. F. Harvey Jacob, a relative of Alfred Webb, the text is now in the Friends' Historical Library, Dublin.

The manuscript is 580 pages in length, and the text contains about 75,000 words. In order to bring the text to an acceptable length for publication, some radical cuts had to be made. Webb wrote at length about his family circle and married life; and by concentrating here on his political life, it has been possible to cut the text to about 20,000 words. The deleted portions are indicated within square brackets with a note on their contents.

I have intervened as little as possible in presenting the text. Occasional misspellings of personal names have been silently corrected, and additional punctuation has occasionally been supplied in order to avoid obscurity. Titles of books and newspapers and the names of ships have been given in italic type. Apart from these minor changes, the original spelling, punctuation, paragraphing and stylistic forms have been retained. Translations, extensions of abbreviations and clarifications have been supplied in square brackets.

Autobiography of Alfred Webb

[Friends' Historical Library, Dublin]

Famine to Business

At home, whilst attending school I worked in the office in leisure hours and earned pocket money. I find by a note of my mother's that Richard set up type at 5 years of age and I at the same time when I was 6½— a fair measure of his superiority in all work, literary or otherwise through life.[1] Some Recollections of early life written by Deborah since the first draft of these Recollections of mine were penned, show also how much clearer her memory is of the events of our early life — even such as to place when I was several years older than she was.[2] At one time I saved up 50s/— and my Father doubling it I bought from Gaskin in College-green, the watch, then second hand which I have worn ever since — 57 years. Johnny Daly and others of the apprentices were my friends. They sometimes worked on into the night — there were then no Factory Acts — and we used to regale ourselves on sumptuous suppers brought in surreptitiously from Townsend-street — penny rolls, pigs crubeens [trotters], a halfpenny worth of 'mixed milk' — half fresh, half butter milk and other like delicacies. Bread well buttered, the buttered side turned down on a hot stove was an especial delicacy. I can still imagine the smell and quiet of the office at those late hours — the snugness of the stove and the gas light. Mother often came out to call me in to bed. We were profoundly moved by the Revolutionary events of 1848; the apprentices and I were pronounced rebels. Johnny Daly matured a plan for the throwing up of barricades, and we promised at all events to stand firmly by each other when we found ourselves in the dock. We composed and printed a little *Life of John Mitchel* — then my special hero — a place he afterwards forfeited in my estimation by his approval of American Slavery.[3] (When I returned from Australia in 1855 I found his portrait in my bedroom taken down.) I have since come to know many of his friends and relatives, in especial Mrs John Martin, his sister.[4] (Lately I gave away some writing of his and his portrait to an enthusiastic admirer, Miss Annie Walsh, a nice Nova Scotia girl, who was some time in Dublin.) What insignificant incidents remain in the mind, whilst really important events are forgotten! Daly and I used to work at a printing press in a window. In the back windows of Crawleys house next to ours — the Crawleys had then gone to Australia — it may have been about 1851 — in these back windows worked some seamstress girls, and sundry kissings of hands used to proceed between us, when their mistress was out of the room. This was in full swing one day when Johnny and I perceived their mistress coming in at the back of the room. They were oblivious to the reason that caused us to apply diligently to our work, until the mistress came behind them and boxed their ears. Daly was the son of a then well known Irish scholar and bookseller living in Anglesea-street. Poor fellow. His father was unkind. He married early and died of consumption. Father used to say if his brain were opened there would be nothing found in it but a fiddle — which instrument he played. Amongst other interesting sojourners in our house about the period of the famine was Asenath Nicholson, from the United States — a pronounced vegetarian and philanthropist.[5] She travelled about Ireland mostly on foot carrying her belongings in a large muff. She wrote little cookery books and stories, and embodied her Irish experiences in *Ireland's Welcome to the Stranger*, a copy of which I have. She much annoyed our servant by cooking in the kitchen. (I shall never forget the delicious Indian meal fritters she concocted — we had never heard of indian meal — or 'yellow male' [corn meal] as our people called it until the famine.)

Butter was her peculiar aversion — a deadly substance. She told a story of her or some friend having examined the intestines of some deceased patient, and finding them choked with butter. Our 'Dunville' cousins then in the north considered she eat too many gooseberries in their garden, and used to pull them, fill them with butter and replace them on thorns on the trees in hopes she would light on them. She sometimes took Richard or me with her in her perigrinations round Dublin.

Mr Heilines, a German, author of a grammar, was over about this time. Our parents took German lessons from him. He had some theory about the round towers. He took me to Clondalkin — the railway had just been opened. Admission to the tower was noted 6½d (half the old Irish shilling of 13 pence) — the 6d very small and the ½d very large. We were disappointed at having to pay 1s/1d instead of one penny. I never shall forget the lusciousness of a penny cake to which the good man treated me at a confectioners on Ushers Quay, next Gawleys — it is only lately the old name O'Hara disappeared over the shop. The next time I ascended the tower was over 50 years later when I cycled there with Bertha Williams, now Baker, and one of her Wright cousins from Belfast.

About this time died our particular friend Catherine Nugent, a woman of remarkable abilities, centre of a literary coterie in Dublin. A Catholic girl, assistant at Newmans, a furriers in Grafton-street, about where Mannings is now, she had been intimate with many of the United Irishmen, and with Shelley and his wife when they were in Dublin.[6] When the Newmans retired from business she lived with them in Baggot-street as a member of their family, and after Mr Newman's death continued as companion to his widow and daughter. Though she never formally abjured Catholicism, she ceased to attend its sacraments, and was broadly liberal. She was a charming companion, endowed with wit and literary taste. Father when a young man had become acquainted with her, I believe through the Downes.[7] The Newmans were the only carriage people we knew. She is buried with the Newmans in St Anne's churchyard — the grave with a German inscription directly outside the glass door from Molesworth-street. After her loss, Miss Newman, left alone, highly educated, brought over from London, a niece of Catherine Nugent's, a neutral, formal lady-like character. Richard and I continued the acquaintance after Fathers death. Miss Newman died. All the family property went to Miss Nugent. In conversation one day she told me they had destroyed a large correspondence of her Aunt with the United Irishmen. She still retained some Shelley correspondence. This she lent to me under promise not to show it to anyone. I copied it privately and after her death published it in the *New York Nation* — putting Professor Dowden in the way of procuring the originals.[8] Catherine Nugent, sen. detested the memory of Shelley on account of his treatment of Harriet. She had no love for O'Connell[9] — it is seldom that people interested in politics carry on their appreciation to persons advocating upon different lines the political opinions they themselves were first enthusiastic about. My sympathy with and action in the Land League movement ended Miss Nugent, Jun['s] friendship for me. But for this I always thought I had a likelihood of inheriting some of her large property. It all went to persons strange to me. I never pass the house in Baggot Street that thoughts of old times do not flood my being.

Richard Dowden, Richard — Professor Dowden's uncle a delightful white-haired Corkonian was an occasional visitor.[10] His hearty laugh announced his presence in the house. My father delighted in him. When the Volunteer movement commenced in England he happened to dine with us in the Kitchen. I remember his saying how certain it was to lead to the rise of war feeling — a forecast too sadly verified.

That strange man, Joseph Barker, was also over. He then edited a radical free thinking paper, *The People*, which had a large circulation in the North of England. We took it regularly for many years. I remember a wild drive, when a Mr Campion, one of his Dublin admirers, took him, Lizzie Poole,[11] and myself to visit the White Quaker Communistic community at Newlands. Campion appeared inclined to drive into every vehicle we met. It was deplorable to see respectable old Quaker ladies barefoot and mixed up with disreputable riff-raff. We interviewed Joshua Jacob himself. He received us in bed in the gate house, which it was his turn to keep. As he spoke to us he shelled corn between his hands.

Barker was originally a Methodist Preacher. Next, when we knew him, Freethinker. Then he took up American land dealing and emigration. I think he was influential in the Suliots emigration.[12] I believe they did not think him altogether straightforward. He ultimately returned to the narrowest orthodoxy, and spent his latter years trying to rescue from perdition the souls he had led astray.

At this period almost any reformer or advocate of new ideas for the regeneration of the world was accepted and received by us. However our parents' sense of light and their strong common sense prevented their being carried away too far as others were. Wherever they suspected laxity in morals or in money matters they were suspicious of the pretensions and of character. My sister reminds me we children called a dog after Joseph Barker.

The White Quakers had separated from Friends in the years before the Famine. Joshua Jacob, a Dublin grocer, and Abigail Beale were the leaders.[13] They claimed to be the real Friends or 'children of light'. Adherents were chiefly drawn from Waterford and Clonmel, amongst them our Great Aunt Waring. They wore white clothes, untanned shoes, and drove about in white painted cars. They carried doctrines regarding the leadings of the inward light and of the importance of forms of dress to a ridiculous extent — they 'ran it into the ground'. They broke up their china and looking-glasses. They were 'divinely inspired' to steal trustee money (for which Joshua Jacob and I believe others were imprisoned). One or two wives were put away and others were taken. Tracts and placards were distributed broadcast, full of disconnected Scriptural ravings, abuse of Friends, protestations of their own sanctity, and claims that they were the true church. Relative was set against relative and family against family. The ebullition was altogether so disgraceful that every effort has naturally been made to cover it up and forget it. Newenham Harvey purposed to write an account of the movement, but was dissuaded on account of the pain it would give relatives and descendants.[14] They established a separate burial ground in Waterford, now occupied by cottage gardens — a few years ago Aunt Elizabeth showed the locality to me. Their plot in

Glassnevin [*sic*] Cemetery was ornamented with a marble relief of an angel ascending to heaven with the inscription that it was the burial place of the 'Followers of Joshua Jacob and Abigail Beale' (when last I was there this plaque had disappeared).

The Community eventually went to pieces — some died, others returned to their relatives. Joshua Jacob became an ordinary member of Society no longer a Friend, and took for his third wife a poor woman, a Catholic. Many of their descendants, Catholics, are in business in the County Dublin.

For years, in private circles and at Friends' parties the vagaries of the White Quakers formed subject for conversation. A constant visitor at our house was Vallis Peet, the first Friend Barrister, when he was studying at College.[15] He was particularly interested in all about them.

[*5,000 words, omitted here, deal with Webb's Quaker relations.*]

School to Australia

We returned from school in the summer of 1850. Our parents desired we should both have the benefit of another year at Dr Hodgson's. Richard alone was willing to avail himself of the chance. For the next three years I closely devoted myself to printing under Father and Robert Chapman.[16] We then worked, as I continued for long years afterwards with Father, in a manner different from most printers of our class — our desk amongst the employees, and ever taking part in all the operations of the business. There was scarcely anything to which we did not lend a hand, and this for 60 hours a week — no Saturday half holiday — often working on the few holidays of the year and often working overtime.

The Famine had compelled attention to the condition of Ireland. The Statistical Society was established about 1847 by Dr Hancock, Dr Ingram, Dix Hutton, John [*recte* Thomas] O'Hagan (afterwards Lord O'Hagan) and other young men, many of whom afterwards sat on the bench. Archbishop Whately was President.[17] Its meetings, held in the Dublin Society House, were most interesting. I was one of its oldest members when 50 years later I ceased attending its meetings. We printed much for this Society, and became intimate with the circle. Father and Mother's unusual critical and literary abilities making his relations with customers different from those of most printers with their clients. Mother helped in proof reading and such office work. Jonathan Pim brought much work.[18] We printed his valuable work *Condition and Prospect of Ireland*, and the *Report of the Relief Committee of the Society of Friends*. Through Messrs Vansens, we printed a number of medical works. James Haughton continued as intimate as ever.[19] Richard Allen began to go off on those evangelical lines which a few years later after the death of his first wife, Anne, so entirely absorbed him.[20] Ireland then, in Gavan Duffy's words, appeared to be a 'corpse on the dissecting table'.[21]

Our sisters attended various schools, and later an admirable Ladies' College in London. It was some years later before our parents ventured to introduce a piano into the house for the girls against the approval (or at first knowledge) of our elder relatives or 'The Overseers' of the Society. For boys the piano was then unthought of in our class, any more than the violin for girls.

The Mutual Improvement Association, established a few years previously by John Edmondson, a real worthy, and others — afterwards merged in the Friends' Institute — was, like the Institute a material educational influence in my life and in our circle. Its first meetings were at the lodgings or houses of its members, then at hired rooms — at this period at 18 Eustace-street, under the aegis of the Institute, then lately started. Thomas and Elizabeth Cole were Librarian and caretaker.[22] In 1861 the two Societies were merged and removed to Molesworth-street. I read my first paper (one on Printing) in 1852, and on the average gave one annually for the next 25 years, and less often since that. I was early on the Committee. The habit of thus forcing myself to arrange my thoughts was a training in itself. I acquired the power of sitting down, whether I liked or not; not that I ever could acquire a good style. I learned to speak, but never with facility. All through life I have attempted and done much that others might have attempted and done better if they had cared to exert themselves. I always had more ideas than power of expression. Our Parents were more than ever involved in the Anti-Slavery controversy. The Mexican War, the Fugitive Slave Act, and other measures of the pro-slavery party to maintain the institution, made the contest increasingly bitter and onerous.[23] They edited the *Anti Slavery Advocate* which we printed, almost entirely at the expense of Dr Estlin of Bristol, who, with his beloved daughter Mary, who became our lifelong friend, were occasionally visitors at our house.[24] She came down laughing one morning. She had brought a lump of camphor as a preventitive of fleas, and had found one sitting on same on her dressing table. Dr Estlin was an eminent oculist in Bristol. These like most of our friends not Friends were Unitarians. The *Advocate* and my Father's general character and untiring effort in so many good causes caused him to be more and more widely known and respected on both sides of the Atlantic. He carried on a wide correspondence. Harriet Martineau and her niece Susan were also our visitors.[25] Father travelled with her and afterwards with her nephews Thomas and Frank Martineau of Birmingham. (Do we not deprive ourselves of much pleasure and benefit at present by not being ready to receive and entertain visitors more simply and naturally as in those days. Upon the other hand might not Mother have lived long past 53 but for the domestic strains that must have been upon her.) In later times Thomas Martineau was a Unionist — Frank a Home Ruler. I stopped at his house and corresponded with him 40 years later.

Miss Martineau was deaf and used a trumpet. Dr Hancock, one of our friends most interested in Irish affairs, visited her at our house. He had the habit of saying 'O aye', 'O aye' when listening to conversation. When he left, she remarked what an intelligent young man he was, and what a pity he was so asthmatic. Dr Hancock was the life and soul of the Statistical Society, and of politico-economic and official efforts for the good of Ireland — an entirely unselfish man. Many, largely through his aid, stepped over his shoulders into high positions. He was great nephew of Samuel Neilson, the United Irishman, and was proud of the relationship.[26] Neilson drank. Dr Hancock's brothers proved sad exemplars of the heredity of the drink craving. Both of them attained fine positions in life, and later utterly lost themselves and ruined their families through drink. He married a daughter of James Haughton. They had no children. His brothers' conduct largely helped to break him down. He became peculiar. The Notice of Neilson in my *Compendium* stands a proof of it — he insisted upon writing it himself. When in printing I came to the name he was not ready, and I had to omit it for the Appendix, and in the end I had to print what I myself had written, helped by a few hints from him. When last I saw him in the late 80's he was a wreck under the care of Dr Eustace, where Joe Poole is.[27] His wife nobly stood by him to the last, living with him in a cottage at Dr Eustace's. He was about the best customer we ever had. The efforts of able and devoted men such as he affected only the surface evils of Ireland. It required the cataclysms of Fenianism[28] and the Land League to bring about radical beneficial reform.

A painful schism arose in the Anti-Slavery party. Religious differences were at the bottom of it. In consequence of the extent to which the Bible was used to defend slavery, and its consequent repudiation as an inspired book by earnest abolitionists, participation in the movement as carried on by the Garrisonian abolitionists — the only really effective movement — was undoubtedly subversive of current orthodoxy. Mr Garrison left the columns of his paper, *The Liberator*, open to the discussion of all subjects.[29] He was the only great reformer I have ever heard of who neither concealed nor shirked opinions on other subjects in deference to what might be considered the importance of maintaining his prestige and influence for the advancement of the object he had most at heart. Difference on this subject was complicated by the question as to whether or not it was right to engage in political action in the United States — The contention of Mr Garrison and his followers, of which our parents were amongst the most enthusiastic was that the constitution of the United States as it stood was on the slavery question 'a compact with Hell'.

Hence arose bitter alienation between many of those who had been our best friends. At the same time many of the enlightened orthodox, such as Eliza Wigham, Mary Edmondson,[30] Elizabeth Pease Nichol, recognizing that slavery was a greater evil than could be any theological differences continued to be our parents hearty coadjutors.

At this period the 'Dunville Webbs' — Wilhelmina, Anna, Maria, William Henry, Charley, and Richard were our closest friends. Their Mother, Maria Webb, was a leader of the Anti-Garrisonians.[31] Many of us were inclined to agree that 'slavery was very bad; but that Anti-Slavery was worse'. Mother read *Uncle Tom's Cabin* to us as it came out in an American newspaper.[32] My Father surmised it would pay to publish in book form. None of us anticipated its world wide popularity or the influence it would have on the slavery question. The 'Dunville Webbs' were children of William Webb and Maria Lamb Webb. He was first cousin of my Grandfather James Webb.[33] Consequently their children were a generation older than we though of the same age. He had come up from Belfast to help his brother-in-law, Richard Allen, who had opened in addition to 52 High-street a new (the present) shop in Sackville-Street. At both places Richard Allen was making money fast on the newly discovered line of ready made clothing and whole-sale advertizing. They first lived in High-Street, then in Dunville-avenue (the house — still standing with the turret on it — but no roads then ran south from Dunville-avenue) — later to Palmerston-road. They were a delightful family. Maria Webb sr. wrote books on the Irish church and Quaker Biography. Wilhelmina married John Webb (his third wife); Anna married Abraham Shackleton. William Henry, our special friend, was drowned in Lough Neagh in 1870. Charley, from nothing, became a wealthy linen manufacturer and one of the leading conservatives in the North. Richard Joined him in partnership and later separated. Maria D. became an artist and married an artist, Henry Robinson. Richard, father of a large family, living in Belfast, and Maria, a childless widow, living in St Ives, alone survive.

One day out walking, our Nannie and Maria bought a little dog. Some one said it was a mongrel, which they interpreted 'Mogul', a specially fine breed. It cost 3d; it had three black spots; it was our third dog. We called it Trio. It was our cherished pet for long years. Finally, surreptitiously following a cab in which Father and Mother were going to a train, it was run over. They brought it back, she lingered not apparently in pain for some days, recognizing us, and licking our hands to the last. I see, almost as vividly as if in reality the corner of the office in which she lingered. We had quite a cemetery of pets in our yard.

Richard, after leaving school, also worked in the printing office. It would have been more just to him if he had been regularly placed at some other business. A new series of apprentices were now in the office. I was intimate with some of them and went for walks with them on Sundays and holidays. It was on a walk to Glencree, that I visited that very old man to whom I referred at an early page. Some of our earlier workers had gone to America. John Lee ran away from his wife, a poor creature. She followed him; and came back after him to Ireland — again to America where she fortunately died. He then married a decent woman, once assistant to Abby Hewson in Athy. His son was the only boy ever called after my father — Richard Davis Webb Lee. My wife and I visited them in New York in 1872. Father had left the lad a small bequest. The parents died later. R. D. W. Lee, a delicate young man came to see us, and stayed with us at Highfield-road. He died of consumption in California.

Our earlier apprentices were generally Protestant, later mixed, and before I gave up business they were I believe all Catholic. At first they were bound by indenture — tied together for seven years. Later this system became more and more repugnant to the spirit of the times and we changed it to one of free service — terminable on a week's notice on either side.

I often visited the Pooles — Aunt Mary and Sarah, now settled with Jacob at Ballybeg.[34] As the Harveys grew up Waterford became more and more attractive. Newenham was younger than I, but cleverer in every way, and even then he had begun to save money, whilst I had saved none, all through he was more intimate with Richard than with me. The younger members of the family were then unborn or in arms. Aunt Elizabeth was the first person with whom I had correspondence on serious subjects and I began to appreciate the real kindness under the reserve and stately manners of the Moores.[35] The then established

Encumbered Estates Court threw much work into our hands.[36] It was believed that the free sale of such estates would settle the land question on a permanent English basis: it made it worse. Till then old relations between landlords and tenants and a regard for old Irish custom somewhat modified the evils of a system where the landlords were placed by the union above the public opinion of the country at large. Most of the new purchasers regarded the tenants merely as machines from whom to obtain the largest amount of rent. Not until long afterwards did I understand why a tenant of Joe Poole's sighed as he signed a lease in Aunt Matty's shop. It was because thus he definitely put himself on contract and outside of old Irish custom of dual ownership. Now began the period of wholesale brutal evictions in Ireland, leading up to Fenianism. But Irish custom and sense of right was able to assert itself in the end — not however until after thirty years more of sorrow. After the Thompsons went to Australia, Willy remained behind at Uncle James.[37] We were much of companions.

A Russian lady, Madame Shtchepoteff, introduced by a friend, appeared in our circle at this time, and continued in it for 10 or 12 years. She was a brilliant pleasant woman, who seemed to become rather less so as the years went by. Her means also became smaller. There was something inscrutable about her — some thought her a Russian spy. During these years she lodged for a time at Mrs Moore's in Manchester. There was a strangeness in her being there robbed out of her locked bag in her bedroom of a considerable sum in gold. She was in many ways a lady and went with us to lectures, and was asked out to parties in our circle. Later, after I was married Lizzie used to complain at the scent of tobacco on her belongings stored with us, from her cigarette smoking. She finally disappeared in the mystery out of which she emerged. Deborah draws my attention to the following stanza in a volume of poetry, opposite which our mother has placed Madame Shtchepoteff's initials:

> 'Oh! tell me of your varied fortunes,
> For you know not from your face,

> Looks out strange sadness, lit with rapture
> And melancholy grace.'

De Vesci Lodge, Monkstown, where lived Uncle James Webb and Aunt Anne, Mary Elizabeth (Tosey) and Lydia Maria (Sissy) was always open to us. Our whole family often spent Sundays there, and at times when they went away — principally to Orange Hill in summer we occupied it. One winter's evening, gathered cozily round the fire, Aunt Anne read to us some of the opening chapters of a new novel by an unknown author that had just appeared — *Jane Eyre*.[38]

And oh the glory and interest of Dickens' and Thackeray's novels coming out in monthly shilling numbers, that Anne Allen used to lend us. Our parents grudged every shilling spent on their own enjoyments.

Richard and Anne Allen had moved from over their shop, 52 High-street, to a beautiful house and grounds, Brooklawn, Blackrock. There they lived in style, and surrounded themselves with beautiful pictures, books, and furniture in a way far beyond the rest of our circle; and, wonder of wonders!, they travelled on the Continent, which none of us ever expected to do — Father had. Anne Allen, William Webb's sister, was a woman of taste, and had read and thought.[39] Both she and her husband were at that time, like others of our circle deeply interested in all reform movements — 'Anti-Everythingarians' — and their house like ours was open to philanthropists and lecturers. There was a certain fastidiousness and vein of selfishness in Anne Allen; but she fully appreciated and greatly loved Mother, at whose feet she was by her own desire buried. At Brooklawn we all often spent delightful Sunday afternoons. There were sumptuous dinners, served round by Christy, the coachman, in white gloves, delicious dessert, tea in the drawing-room, and a wealth of books and pictures. At one of these dinners — this is going back a few years — Richard Allen produced and read the latest number of Mitchel's *United Irishman*.[40] Sometimes, for my health, I was kindly asked out there to sleep, returning home early in the morning before breakfast so as to be in time for the opening of the office. Richard Allen was a devoted husband. One summer's morning I found him out in the grounds rubbing two pieces of bone across each other, to lead Anne to suppose there were plenty of corncrakes about, of which she was fond. Few people, each in their own way excellent could be much more different than Richard Allen's two wives — the somewhat exclusive refined Anne, and the expansive Evangelical Mary Anne, who filled the house with preachers and Sunday School teachers.

Many were the late and weary tramps we all had in those days from De Vesci Lodge and Brooklawn to Blackrock Station on Sunday evenings. The stations were all open, and a return or single to Booterstown or Blackrock carried one on as far as one wished to Kingstown or Monkstown. Once in the train it was lawful to go as far as it went itself.

Passing down Fowne's-street in the course of this recopying I was reminded of Maunders bread shop in that street and the wonderful almost monopoly of sale that firm then had of their bread in Dublin — which was certainly delicious — so crusty fresh and crisp. They delivered no bread, they gave no credit, and the rule in their shops was that you laid down the money on the counter before the bread was handed over.

Benjamin Whitten, an old time friend was in the days of which I am now writing manager & salesman of Maunders in Fowne's-st. In his little rooms over the shop he had got together a collection of paintings which he supposed to be by the Old Masters, and which he was proud to show to Friends, young women especially, at Yearly Meeting and other times. It was about this period, either before or after I went to school, that I was one Saturday sent out to procure change of a £10 note, and lost it. I foolishly delayed on the way to buy apples at a stand by our gate. Probably I lost it then — anyhow those who kept it shortly afterwards went to America. I went thro' untold misery. I had nothing to repay it with. For days I kept away as much as possible from the presence of my Father. And I then acquired the habit, which I have lost only within last few years, of constantly feeling my pockets and saying over to myself a formula: 'Watch, knife, pencil, money, keys, pocket-book.' I used to be amused at finding myself saying this even in Parliament.

The Society of Friends as a peculiar body still shone in (unconsciously) fading glories. Yearly and Quarterly meetings were still great occasions, when town was crowded with Friends young and old in standing collars, immaculate gowns and shawls and Friends' bonnets. Still those coming up to Dublin were as a matter of course lodged at the houses of their friends and relatives, and none would have been allowed to take meals or refreshment at an eating house or confectioners. Such places as our present restaurants, DBC's, Bewley's and the like were not general for 25 years later. We were far behind the Continent and America in such matters. Mr Garrison once told me that in London in the early 40's the only place where a lady could be served with a meal was in a privately engaged room in a hotel. After we left Brunswick-st in 1870 my father and I used to have to dine in a public house. Tea was served at a few confectioners.

Friends' parties then consisted of bringing together as large a number as possible, serving them with tea and cakes and letting them talk, with perhaps some stupid games for the young people and of course much sublatent love making. In the lighter houses, such as ours and Dunville-avenue, charades began to come in some what later, and were a great delight — except to the hosts who had to settle up afterwards. 'Post Office', 'What is it like', 'Consequences' were amongst the games generally played. With giddy young people 'forfeits' were common but not generally encouraged. Friends' interests then lay little outside the Society, and within it they had more in common than now. A Friend to every Friend was supposed as a matter of course to be a friend.

I was then beginning to think less of boats and more of girls. Oh! the glory of those Yearly Meetings (often lasting 9 days) and Quarterly Meetings! Young Friends now can have no conception of what they were. The Shackleton girls would be up from Ballitore and our Waring cousins from Ballinclay and Pooles from Growtown and Sparrows from Wexford; and we boys would have to sleep on 'Shakedowns' on the lobbies. At Uncle Johns[41] in Queen-square would be 70 to tea in a house to which no Friend's family would now invite more than a dozen. We young men and lads would be sent about the square borrowing chairs. Many would sit on the stairs. Seeing that everyone shook hands with everyone on arrival and departure there would not be much fewer than 9700 shake-hands on such an occasion

Balsam poplars then hung over St Mark's churchyard wall — there were then no railings there — and flourished in Queen-square. Their delicious scent always recalls to me those Spring gatherings.

The extravagances of the White Quakers undoubtedly hastened the abandonment by Friends of peculiarities of dress and language.

Through those years I devoted much of my leisure to Irish archae-ology. Petrie's book on the Round Towers had placed the study on a sane basis. The Ordnance Survey then being completed had thrown a flood of light on Irish Topography. The Four Masters had been trans-lated by O'Donovan. The splendid works of the Archaeological, Celtic and Ossianic Societies were appearing.[42] The movement was largely confined to the educated and 'better classes'. While the pre-sent Gaelic movement relies more upon the masses. I read everything I could borrow, and amongst other copying transcribed into a volume for reference all the passages in the Four Masters relating to Round Towers. In this connection I visited most scenes of historic and archaeological interest round Dublin as far north as Tara — especially the valley of the Boyne, and south as far as Bray. I sketched ruins, and wrote papers for the Institute. To these excursions on foot I devoted my time. This taste led to more extended excursions in after years. Although now a Life Member, through cooption, without pay-ment, (as Author of a *Compendium of Irish Biography*,)[43] of the Archae-ological Society of Ireland, I never attend its meetings or excursions, and take little interest in its proceedings. The smashed ruins and everything connected with our history is depressing to me. My inter-ests lie in the fate and fortunes of our people, and in the politics and future of Ireland.

After my return from School I made a few days pedestrian tour in the county of Wicklow with Willy Thompson and a friend of his. Never shall I forget the solemn elation with which we walked up the Valley of

Glendalough, and caught sight of the hoary tower and churches. (I have
still copies of the pamphlet in which I gave an account of the Co. Wicklow portion of this tour.)[44] By myself I walked on in stages to Waterford. Many another excursion had I in after years to Glendalough and
other spots in the county — often walking the whole way from Dublin.
But never again was I impressed as in 1850. The round tower was without its cap till the early 60's. Upon one occasion I visited the place with
Charley Webb and Sam Young. They set fire to the collection of twigs
and old birds nests in the tower. It smoked like a factory chimney, the
neighbours congregated and we were glad to escape.

At one period or another through after years I ascended most of the
important mountains in the county, generally alone. My interest was
great in all localities connected with '98. In later years I took some of
our apprentices for a couple of days walk through the mountains —
used only to Dublin, they were surprised to find that the roads were
not lighted at night.

On another occasion from Belfast I explored the Antrim coast, the
Giants Causeway, and Derry. At this time and for years later I never
thought of stopping at a hotel. I sought out humble lodgings in private
houses and never met anything that was unpleasant. At Belfast I stopped
with the Lambs at Devis View. I had the great honour of being introduced to Miss McCracken at her own house. She had accompanied her
brother to the foot of the scaffold in 1798.[45]

Even then in 1852 Belfast still cherished much of its old pre-Union
liberal traditions. John Lamb was then well known on account of his
letters on the state of the country and the crops. William, Sophia and
Lucy were pleasant companions.

[*In 1853 Webb travelled to Australia, partly for the sake of his health. He lived
in Melbourne for some months, and then he and a friend worked on clearing the
bush and building wooden bridges at Port Fairy, 190 miles west of Melbourne.
Before he returned to England he walked from Melbourne to Sydney, a distance
of about 500 miles. He sailed back to England in May 1855, serving his turn
on the watch and taking lessons in steering.*]

Political and Public Life generally up to end of 1889

I was tolerably active in different philanthropic and reform movements
in my time — temperance, women suffrage, anti C[ontagious]
D[iseases] Acts, Church-disestablishment and others. Those which have
most roused my enthusiasm were those concerning people oppressed
that could not help themselves — such as slaves, women deprived of
the franchise, the Indian people, practically without a voice in the government of their own country — the Chinese with the use of opium
almost forced on them. I regard the wars waged by England to keep
open the opium trade with China as the greatest (in their consequences)
political crimes ever committed.[46] The total massacre of populations
by the Romans was less barbarous than the aiding in planting a vice like
opium smoking in the vitals of a people.

Drink though perhaps the worst of all evils in these countries never
roused my enthusiasm against it in proportion to its enormity. For this
reason. That its use is deliberately held to by those fully informed and
who are free agents. They have a right to drink if they wish; even the
Irish people if they really desired could scotch the traffic in Ireland. I
can feel no enthusiasm in trying to persuade people to do their duty by
themselves.

The first object in which I attended public meetings and spoke a little
was the effort to open Stephen's green to the public, which then failed.[47]
The evidence of conservatives that our people would make a waste of it
put in was so strong that Parliament would not pass our bill. I went to
London in aid of it — it was Lizzie's and my first visit to London
together (about 1865) — but was not thought a sufficiently strong wit-
ness, and was not examined. My principal coadjutors in this were John
McEvoy, Solomons the optician, and a young man whose name I forget,
a clerk in the employ of the corporation — he used always in his
speeches to bring in the words: 'are we not all working men?' — Now
these words bring back his name — Nugent Robinson.[48] He afterwards
embezzled and ran away to America. Solomons used then to attach to
his advertizements 'Works at Denbeigh-place, London'. But McEvoy on

one of his visits went to see the works and found it was only a private house where Solomons' Father lived. John McEvoy was a pudgy little man once extremely active in Dublin affairs. I used to have much to do with him. Lizzie never forgave his once borrowing a pair of rugstraps and returning only one of them. He gradually turned into a conservative — opposing the Corporation bringing in the Vartry Water[49] (he even persuaded me it would be the ruin of the city), and making out that England was unfairly taxed as compared to Ireland. He was a nominal Catholic and kept a chandlers shop in Kingstown. He now lives in London. One evening when I was going to a 'Stephen's-Green' public meeting, Abraham Shackleton happened to be at our house. He then lived in Ballitore. It was perhaps his first introduction to that city life in which he afterwards bore such a part. He came with me 'to see what such a meeting was like'. In those days I became acquainted with T. W. Russell.[50] He was Secretary of a Temperance Association on the committee of which Uncle Thomas Webb and I worked. No one was ever truer to the Temperance cause than Uncle Thomas.[51]

I took a prominent part in the agitation for Disestablishment of the Church in Ireland. Surprisingly few Protestants had the courage to brave Protestant opinion on the subject. I was one of the Secretaries that inaugurated a meeting of Protestants in favour of the change. There was a small attendance and we were broken up before we could get to business by a Protestant mob who threw brickbats at us on the platform. My fellow secretary was a J. A. Mowatt,[52] then a prominent temperance advocate. He was a clever man, but was too fond of speaking at length in a somewhat harsh voice upon every subject at every kind of meeting. I was then beginning to take part in the proceedings of the Statistical Society — I had already read a paper there — I believe I was on the council later. Poor Mowatt, an earnest, well intentioned man, was near breaking up the Society by his numerous and protracted speeches.

I have now cleared the way for some short particulars of my connection with Irish National politics, which from 1865 onwards became one of the chief factors in my life. Ireland for 25 years onward was, as it often had been before, practically in a state of revolution; and in that revolution I took a part, as far as my conscience and abilities would allow, regardless of my own material interests, and contributing from time to time as much as I was able — £100 in a lump upon more than one occasion. The part I took was not sufficiently important ever to be recorded in history. Mr Davitt mentions me in his *Fall of Feudalism*; but then I am his personal friend.[53] It was more my conviction and earnestness, and the fact of my being a Protestant — regarded as being a Friend, tho I never claimed the appellation — it was more these than any special ability, that gave me even such prominence as came to be assigned me. Neither in this nor in any other phase of my active life did I contribute anything of value in the way of initiative. My abilities have been for the most part executive — those of a disciple not of a leader.

I am not going to write a history of those times. Nor shall I make any real use of diaries (now at second writing of these recollections available) — they would lead me into trivialities and unnecessarily prolong my narrative. Fenianism was an effort to sever the connexion with Gt Britain and establish an Irish Republic. If success had been possible it would have been a justifiable movement. Coming to understand the reasons and motives of the leaders, I came to sympathize with them, just as abolitionists and peace lovers sympathized with John Brown's raid,[54] and as 'all Ireland' does with Emmet. 'To understand is to pardon.' I need not explain what Home Rule means.

The Parnell–Biggar policy of violence and obstruction in Parliament was entirely justifiable — the only means by which it was possible to force the attention of that assembly to Irish affairs.[55]

Boycotting without violence is an entirely justifiable weapon of offence and defence. We all resort to it. War for the attainment of Land Reform in Ireland, would have been justifiable in the estimation of men of unbiassed minds, who believed war or revolution under any circumstances in the worlds history justifiable. Before the stolid ignorance and indifference of Parliament reason had been exhausted. Before Parnell and Davitt took the matter in hands, Jonathan Pim, who had more than any man given himself to the constitutional agitation and exposition of the question, admitted to me that he saw no chance of a settlement. Ireland's patience was exhausted. There was doubtless violence in the policy of the Land League — rather deliberate shutting of eyes to violence, without which it was felt, and rightly felt, the movement could not succeed. And an inevitable outcome of rousing a people to the realization of their wrongs and an assertion of their rights is violence to an extent and a degree never contemplated by those who set the ball rolling. The Reformation for a time threw central Europe into chaos. My belief is, there never was a movement other than the Land League movement in Ireland, that against greater odds with less suffering all round conferred greater benefits on a people. It was opposed by most of the education and wealth in Ireland. The Protestant tenantry coldly stood aside and let others fight the battle, yet were the first to avail themselves of victory, as have done thousands of those who openly opposed. The much abused and much despised Land League movement raised the condition of the tenantry of Ireland from that of serfs to that of freemen. Well has Mr Davitt entitled his history of the movement *The Fall of Feudalism*.

The Church Establishment in Ireland was a grotesquely hideous wrong. It also was supported by the wealth, 'intelligence' and education of Ireland. Nine Protestants out of ten were in its favour. A mere handful even of Friends were against it. Nothing but the Fenian storm would have brought it down and the then existence in England of Liberal traditions since given to the winds.

Broadly regarding them the 'wealth' the 'education' the 'respectability' the 'higher education' of Ireland — all that is called 'society' — set itself resolutely against all the reforms of the past 50 years — reforms now generally acknowledged to have been necessary and which have contributed to the elevation and happiness of all classes remaining in the island. Really to sympathize with and aid those reforms as I and others of my class did necessitated the sacrifice for the time of much that was sweetest in life.

My churchism, my bachelor days, my marriage, mother's death, the American War tended somewhat though not entirely to dim the National proclivities of my youth. We read *Saunders* a conservative paper, and the

English journals, such as the *Spectator*. We began to hear much of the Fenians, regarding them as a pestilent set of ruffians set upon murdering Protestants and landlords. I went down to Cork in the autumn of 1865 to look after a business or partnership — the printing being depressed at that time. There the young Addeys[56] pointed me out a prison which they said was full of Fenians.[57] I gave but lazy attention to the information. Upon my return Father's angina-pectoris developed and it was impossible for me to think of leaving Dublin. Fenian trials came on. Father was summoned as a juror. I attended with a medical certificate of his unfitness. It was one of the last days of November or first of December, 1865. There in the Dock from which Emmet and the Shearses had gone to execution I saw men there, who from the evidence, their demeanour and their speeches before conviction were evidently as great and pure intentioned men as were any of those of '98. I heard O'Leary, Luby and Kickham,[58] all three afterwards my friends either personally or by correspondence, condemned to 20 years endurance of a system of punishment the most barbarous, next to the application of the rack or the thumb screw, perhaps ever invented by human ingenuity, by a judge, Keogh,[59] who had but a few years previously climbed to place by profession of the very principles they put in practice. Under the laws of Statesmen and a people who a few years previously had been exclaiming against Austrian dungeons in Italy.[60] And they were but a few of those condemned in like manner. (I cannot forget an incident in these trials that shows how personal habit persists through all circumstances in life. Luby as the judge was sentencing him, remarked a speck of dust on his coat and flicked it off with a fillip of his finger and thumb.) I felt there must be something radically wrong, as there was, in a state of things when such men could thus rise up and submit themselves to such a doom. Like Paul on his road to Damascus a sudden light shone on my mind and I left Green-street Court House a changed man. For the second time in my life an experience altered the current of my thoughts and affected all my after life. What I went through in succeeding years was only equalled 35 years later when I had to live through the slow agony and ultimate ruin and extinction by these countries of the South African Republics.

We visited and made friends with the families of prisoners. We got to know Mrs Luby and her children. I was honoured with the friendship of John O'Leary's sister, a beautiful character.[61] Some of my letters in the *Manchester Examiner* and the *Daily News* attracted attention. For some years by an annual subscription, we maintained the boy and girl of a poor man who was shot, in a Catholic orphanage. After the Manchester Rescue I secretly printed a number of memorial cards and sold them for the benefit of the families of Allen, Larkin and O'Brien.[62] I attended Amnesty meetings and became well known in nationalist circles.[63]

My principal Nationalist friends at that time were the Brothers Sullivan[64] who edited *The Nation*, and the most widely read Nationalist paper of the period, the *Weekly News*. I also knew Richard Pigott,[65] and wrote occasionally for his paper *The Irishman*. I saw Sullivan with Pigott in prison for their articles on the execution of the Manchester Martyrs. Pigott later came down in the world, and used to apply to me for assistance. He it was that forged the *The Times* letters, and shot himself in Spain.

The Sullivans were familiarly known by the initials of their Christian names — A.M., T.D., D.B., and D. A.M. was the ablest of the three [*sic*] a fine writer and speaker. When in Parliament he espoused all good causes. Latterly he devoted himself more and more to Temperance and before his death, discouraged by the violence of the Parnell movement, came to place it almost before Home Rule. His wife, a charming woman, still a worker in Temperance and Women Suffrage was a Southerner. A.M.'s sympathies in the [American Civil] War were consequently on the side of the South. He wrote an admirable *Story of Ireland*, and published many useful books. I was so delighted with a speech in Parliament of A.M. on the Zulu war that I printed a number for gratuitous distribution. His desire to please sometimes laid him open to the charge of disingenuousness. Our Home Rule secretary, Captain Dunn,[66] once asked him to interest himself in someone's case. 'Write me a letter with full particulars.' Captain Dunn did so. The following day he met A.M. and asked him if the letter would do. 'Oh! yes, first rate, it is all right' he rejoined. 'The very thing.' When Dunn reached our office our porter met him with a long face to say he had forgotten to post letters the previous evening, and handed them to him, that to A.M. amongst them.

T.D. was and is a poet, the author of 'God Save Ireland'. While Lord Mayor he suffered imprisonment as a person of bad character. He was long in Parliament. I received a letter from him as I wrote the previous page. He and I are, so far as I know, the only members alive of a connection with the management of the Home Rule movement in its earlier years. D.B. became a lawyer and kept rather on the outskirts of politics. He did well, kept a yacht, but I believe is now addicted to drink. He was lately a member of the Waterford Bridge Commission. D., the least talented of the brothers, through all differences keeps his seat in Parliament — saying little and closely attending. The life suits him and he suits it.[67]

The Sullivans and their cousins W. M. Murphy and T. M. Healy, all came from Bantry, and were known as the 'Bantry gang'.[68] Extreme nationalists harboured a suspicion of them all along. This prejudice in later years, and since A.M.'s death has been justified even to moderate nationalists. If Healy and Murphy had had their way the national movement would have been brought to an end. It is much to be regretted that family sympathy carried T.D. out of Parliament with his cousin W.M.M. Some curious characters floated on the surface of the early as of later movements.

There was Tommy Reid, more or less of a dwarf, with short legs — I still see him about town — a provoking humorous little man, whose real opinions it was not easy to divine. He delighted to orate at elections and on all possible occasions. He used to draw down thunders of applause from the populace.

There was Mr Barnes, a lawyer of good means, who would force himself into meetings; and if once gained a hearing, it was all but impossible to stop him.[69] He distributed handbills and tracts by the thousand, the subject of which, as well as of his orations was his own merits and importance. He did not much care on which side a meeting or demonstration was, so long as he could obtain a hearing. If he entered a bus — it was before the days of trams, he immediately began to speak in a loud voice, addressing himself to any unfortunate person he knew — such as myself, until he had to leave. Many a time upon such occasions did I wish myself at the other side of the world. For naturally the other passengers thought I was particeps criminis [partner in crime]. Then there was Matthew More Donagh Keilly, otherwise 'the man with the big feet', who in the end was sure to come for an order for coals to everyone to whom he was introduced or whose name he came to know. A tall, shambling, bald-headed rosey faced man, dressed in black, with a silk hat, and for whom 'herring-boxes, without topses' would have well-served for 'sandals'. He was a flaming nationalist. At meetings he would stand in a prominent place on the platform, and at demonstrations and processions he would occupy a vantage ground, where he would solemnly wave his hat like a Catherine-wheel, and elicit shouts of approbation from the crowd, who must often have mistaken him for the O'Donoghue himself, or Isaac Butt.[70]

Rise of Home Rule to my despair in 1878

The Home Government Association, afterwards the Irish Home Rule League was established in May, 1870, and I was one of the first to join.[71] After the hopeless agony of the previous years, it appeared to me like the opening of the gates of heaven. I thought in my innocence that such a reasonable movement, such a great cause would gradually gather strength and march to assured victory as had the Anti-Corn Law League and the Anti-Slavery Society. Amongst those in our circle who soon joined were my Father, John Chandlee, Edmund Harvey and Thomas H. Webb.

The movement at first was principally composed of Protestant conservatives piqued at the Disestablishment of the Church. There were numbers of clergymen, such as Canon Carmichael, afterwards one of our bitterest opponents. Even a year afterwards, the *Irish Times*, *Mail*, *Saunders* and other conservative Irish-Dublin papers were on our side.

They must have dreamed of an Irish Parliament in which they would have the upper hand as before the Union. I soon came to the front, was in truth one of the most earnest and active members and was appointed a kind of subsidiary Hon. Secretary.

Under the influence of English papers Father gradually withdrew. Indeed he became anxious at my earnestness and for the fate of the business. So that his name should not be involved in any possible misfortune he insisted it should be taken down and 'Alfred Webb' substituted. This was only a few months before his death.[72] After that event I went back to the old style of 'R. D. Webb and Son', not only, it must honestly be said, out of affection for the old name, but as far as could be to cloke and save the business from too much connection with me in the course, so deadly unpopular with our class of customers, which I was determined to pursue.

I was one of the Hon. Secretaries at the several days Home Rule convention of November 1873, where we had a good array of MP's.[73] Swift MacNeill was one of the earliest of our members.[74]

Isaac Butt was chairman and inspirer of the movement. He was a strange mixture of spiritual devotion, moved by the sacrifices of the Fenians to a high ideal for Ireland, and of gross materialism and vanity. His portrait in the National Gallery is one of the best I ever saw of men I have known.[75] He was unreliable in money matters. Pope's line on Bacon in a minor degree applied to him,

'The wisest, brightest, meanest of mankind!'[76]

Once leaving his house after dinner I was shocked to find on the doorstep a poor woman vainly seeking payment for some viand she had supplied to our feast. He came late into meetings for the pleasure of listening to the applause his arrival evoked. I remember his once insisting upon our holding an open-air meeting in a most unsuitable locality near Glasnevin solely so that in the course of his speech he could draw attention to the fact that 'the tower proudly rising above the ashes of O'Connell looks down upon us'. There was beautiful love between him and his son Robert who accompanied him everywhere, and whose career in the army he had ruined by getting him to endorse bills which never were met. He owed money to everyone, amongst others to Uncle Thomas for shoes. He would of course see no creditor. Uncle Thomas was joyfully ordered up stairs when he sent up the name 'Mr Webb.' Whether he ever got his money I do not know.

There were numbers of fine and loveable men connected with the agitation — Professor Galbraith and John Martin in especial.[77] Almost a love grew up between Galbraith and myself — the gold fountain pen which I use occasionally and which I take out to write the remainder of this page in his memory was given me by him. I brought him a stick from America. He was always cheerful and good humoured tho' he had had many domestic trials. He sacrificed a great position for the cause, and was one of the few that accompanied us on into the Parnell movement. I have somewhat the feeling of love and reverence for him that I had for my Father. Their portraits hang near each other in my dining-room.

Mitchell Henry, then reputed millionaire, was one of our great guns, a man of very different stamp.[78] He built Kylemore Castle, and there was very civil to Lizzie and myself when we were at Leenane. We were a strange company sleeping at Mr Armstrong's lodge and boating and driving together — Mr Armstrong, a keen man of business ('Corvane & Co') his son, now head of the firm, Professor Mahaffy,[79] Lizzie and I. In our little parlour at Shamrock Lodge we entertained at breakfast such men as John Martin, M. Henry, S. MacNeill, and John Francis Maguire,[80] the biographer of Father Mathew.[81] His series of articles, collected in pamphlet form on Home Rule, is one of the best treatises ever issued on the subject. Many of those with whom I then worked afterwards turned round & entered the government service — they succumbed to the temptations deliberately offered to detach them from their country's cause — such men as King-Harman and John O. Blunden,[82] fellow Secretaries with me at the conference, and even P. J. Smyth[83] who had planned Mitchel's escape from Tasmania. On the other hand, young men like John Dillon[84] were coming into politics.

O'Neill Daunt, an old '48 man and friend of O'Connell, was for a time our Secretary.[85] An interesting personality on our platforms was old Dr Grattan of Carbury — he had lost one arm in a threshing machine. He was the author of a remarkable book that had much interested Father *On the Human Mind*.[86] He was often passed off on audiences as a son of Grattan. He must have been born long before the Union. When once started it was not easy to stop him, and as he could seldom be heard beyond the platform his intervention in debate tended to the dissolution of a meeting. But I would never stop if I followed out all my recollections connected with the agitation. We first met in Grafton-street, corner of Chatham-street where there is now a fruit shop. Then we moved to Chambers over a Horse Repository on the site of which McKendles in Brunswick-st now stands. Of course opponents vowed we met in a stable. Horse Repositories, where persons put up their horses when in town, were then more common than now. Every one knew Dycers in Stephens Green. In our Gt Brunswick street there were two — Clarendons, over which we met, and Farrells opposite, the site of which is now Tara-street.

Upon one occasion Galbraith, I, and a number of others went down to a banquet with the Archbishop of Tuam.[87] The wild crowd that came to meet us at the railway station became so excited as we approached the residence of His Grace, that they preceded, and we brought up the rear. The banquet was in old Irish style. The potatoes were brought in sheets carried between two women, and the table was so crowded with viands, we had to put some of the dishes on the ground beside our feet, so as to have room to eat anything. 'Is it not interesting to think,' remarked a young man beside me, 'that the eyes of all Europe are fixed on us at present!' This young man — his name escapes me — had been a Fenian. He was an eloquent speaker. For a time served under Parnell. He afterwards became a Whig, and then somewhat of a Healyite.

Meanwhile our cause had apparently been flickering down. It took no real hold on the country. I became more and more despondent. Even Galbraith admitted to me that perhaps seven years was enough for us to have served with little prospect of success. The private utterances of two friends contributed to my discouragement. Dr Lyons was then

Home Rule MP for Dublin.[88] I met him out walking one day and we entered into conversation on the subject ever uppermost in my thoughts. 'The English will never grant us Home Rule, depend upon it,' he said. Dr Gray was an old Repealer and '48 man. The most prominent man in Dublin at the time, knighted for his carrying through of the Vartry Water Scheme.[89] Although not actually a member of our League he posed as an ardent Home Ruler, and gave us help at elections. He owned and edited *The Freeman*, which after the defection of other papers, continued our able advocate and supporter. Late one night we returned together in a cab from an election meeting. In the course of conversation, perhaps as a hint to curb my anticipations, he said: 'We shall have no Home Rule.' These two utterances so stamped themselves on my mind at the time that if I lived 100 years and preserved my intellects I would remember the spots where I heard them — the one on a little bridge half a mile beyond Rathfarnham, the other in the cab as we turned up out of Rathmines into Rathgar-road. If Ireland did not care to pull herself together for a real fight against such difficulty, what was the use in continuing a moribund agitation? We could not change. Ireland had better go her own decadent road.

I wrote a series of letters to the *Freemans Journal* October–November 1878 on these lines of thought. They attracted considerable attention all over the Kingdoms, and were by many hailed as premonition that the troublesome Home Rule question was dead and buried. I received congratulations from old friends such as Dr Hodgson who had mourned my fall into Irish Nationalism. They could not understand that my own convictions were as decided as ever. But however clear my ideas were on the subject, however well intentioned my motives I should not have written those letters. A dislike to occupy an undecided indefinite position is one of the faults of my character. I should have entertained a sentiment I later noticed expressed in an extract in Father's hand from some writer: 'It is never well to discourage an effort for National liberty.' My cousin Thomas Henry took my place as practically Treasurer of the Home Rule League as he afterwards took my place as business adviser of the Parnellite Party after The Split.

Sometime before this one day when I reached the office, Mr Galbraith said, 'a young country gentleman has just been here, anxious to join us. I do not think very much of him but we must see how far we can utilize his apparent desire to serve.' Later the same day he pointed him out to me in Nassau-street. This young man got into Parliament. At some banquet, he and I as of lesser note sat together 'below the salt'. He very earnestly expounded to me a plan of Parliamentary action by which, if he could persuade others to join he hoped they could force attention to Irish questions.

After the appearance of my letters, he came to my office in Abbey-street, sat in an arm chair which I have here now in my house, and said in effect 'Mr Webb you are perhaps a dangerous man to speak to, honest as you are. I have read your letters. I now mean to try with the help of others to bring about a different state of affairs to that which you deplore — we shall see the outcome.' This young man was Charles S. Parnell.[90]

Parnellism

Mr Parnell superseded Mr Butt as Leader. And Mr Butt soon after died. An active Parliamentary Policy, and the establishment of the Irish National Land League shortly followed.[91]

I tried to satisfy myself in our sweet home life at Highfield-road, my walks with 'Lady', my books and studies, our glorious Continental tours, and business. I felt how mistaken those conservative friends were who congratulated me on being clear of the 'disgusting nationalists'. On the other hand A. M. Sullivan had said to me, 'You think you are clear of the movement. You never were more mistaken. With your deep down convictions, you are sure to come back into touch with it.' And he was right. Two years did not pass until I was swept back into it. I attended and spoke at the Land Convention of 1880.[92] I could not actually join the Land League. There was too much said and done which I could not approve, but which yet, with their experiences it was right for others to say and do. After all there was not much difference — no more than there is between the action of Friends who disapprove of war, and yet lend money to carry it on, or that there was between Phineas' disapproval of George's shooting, and his pushing the wounded man into the chasm with the words, 'Friend, thee is not wanted here.'

Archbishop Whately wrote a pamphlet to show that, from the inherent impossibility of his Story, Napoleon could never have been more than a mythical personage.[93] So might a pamphlet be written concerning the history of those days in Ireland.

'In the game that passed' I took 'my hand'. Never it is true a very important one except to myself. Fully 1000 men, women, and children at one time or another, without any process of law known in England passed through our prisons. Visiting prisons became an ever weekly duty. There I saw many times Parnell, Healy, Davitt, Kenny, W. Redmond, A. Kettle, Dillon and others too numerous to mention.[94]

I fully expected myself to be arrested. Nothing but that it did not suit the rôle of the government to add to the number of Protestants of my class, saved me. I have attended meetings where I felt I was so likely to be arrested that I brought biscuits in pocket to eat in the police cell. I often had to speak at meetings under the eyes of government reporters and files of police. I remember one occasion in particular when we thus met in a field in deep snow.

Lately, in looking over some papers I came upon a power of attorney over all my business and property, which I at this time had prepared and executed in favour of my wife in the probable eventuality of my imprisonment.

The murder of the Secretaries dashed high hopes for a time.[95] It was a lovely spring morning, Sunday when going in to yearly meeting the crowds of newsboys on Portobellow [*sic*] bridge attracted our attention and we learned of the tragedy. (If fifty Secretaries had been murdered in England, all England would not have been subjected to the disabilities imposed upon us by the action of irresponsible persons outside the agitation.) It was a crime; but no greater than that of Charlotte Corday or of those who have blown up a Russian Emperor or Grand Duke, or of those who joined in the attempt to assassinate Napoleon III and were acquitted and in truth applauded in England.

On hearing the news a party of us met at the Mansion House and telegraphed to Parnell and others in London, just released from prison, the desirability of the issue of some manifesto. I got my men together, we were up all night and in the morning had 10,000 copies of the Address signed by Parnell, Davitt and Dillon ready for distribution all over Ireland.

James Carey's career was an extraordinary one in the course of the following few months.[96] I never liked the man and had refused to attend meetings called by him. Within that time he sat beside me in fur-lined mantle and cocked hat in the Dublin Corporation. He secretly participated in the crime: was with others arrested: turned approver: hung his friends: was secretly smuggled out of the country: was himself assassinated; and was buried in the sands of Port Elizabeth — all in the course of a few months.

I was a couple of years in the Corporation and on the Port and Harbour Board. I resigned my seat because of the utterly unworthy man our Party selected as Lord Mayor.[97] Abraham Shackleton was also on the Corporation and worked closely with me those years. He was deprived of his JP'ship for both city and county for his action and speeches on our behalf.

I was one of the hardest workers in getting up the Exhibition of 1882.[98] I saw so many poor people lose money in consequence of the manner in which that exhibition was boomed by the national press, that I determined never again to have to do with an undertaking of the kind. Besides the labours and responsibilities nearly killed me.

No one loves and longs for peace and quiet more than I. My convictions were constantly urging me into positions against my natural desire. I have sometimes thought of one of the Napiers' experiences in his first battle as often applicable to me in a mental sense. His knees knocked together, and he addressed them with, 'Ah! my fine fellows, if you knew where I was bringing you, you would be twice as bad.'

When the Irish National League was formed in 1882, I was appointed one of the Treasurers, as it turned out, the acting one.[99]

(Before this on an occasion when there appeared a chance of the government seizing the funds of the Land League, sums, which by the appearance of the rolls of notes may have been tens of £1000s were placed in my safe.) Once I had to draw out all and keep it personally, for fear of government interference. Mr Parnell telegraphed me to do this. Eventually, not being able to stand Parnell's autocratic arrangement about funds, I gave up the position and retired into the ranks of speakers, and those who took the chair at meetings. 'Your leaving may cost the League the loss of many £1000s' remarked Healy to me on the occasion. This, from what I have since heard may have proved literally true. A person into whose hands the management fell during our election, got off to America with some £10,000 — such was the magnitude of the transactions, and the looseness of management attendant on the exigencies of the situation in those days.

At one period when the men were all in prison the women had to take up the running and the Ladies Land League was formed.[100] I gave them what assistance I could. I then became acquainted with Hannah Lynch and Katherine Tynan (now Mrs Hinkson) afterwards well known as Writers.[101] There were several of the Lynch girls — fine women connected with the movement.

I sometimes printed documents secretly at night, a watch kept at a window, so that if the police came we could burn the printing matter before they could effect an entry.

Anna Parnell[102] was once nearly getting me into prison for the possession and care of documents I could not approve. She had me take charge of them on the representation that they were simply 'books'. Her brother, Mr Parnell afterwards expressed to me his regret and disapproval of her action.

The ridiculous was sometimes combined with the tragic and serious. At a time when the leading Lady Land Leaguers were looked upon as Joans of Arc and their subordinate clerks as working themselves to the bone, I called into their offices — the same as those of the U[nited] I[rish] League where I spend part of most days.[103] The principals were out. I looked into the clerks' room, and there they were, a long row of them sitting one behind the other, each engaged in combing out the back hair of the girl before her.

A street incident may illustrate the temper prevalent in Ireland at the time. As I passed some railings dangerous to climb upon I saw a little girl disporting herself. 'Come down out of that' said a passing policeman. 'Yah!' answered the little one, 'Take me, do, I'd l-o-v-e to be in prison.'

I was constant in letter-writing in Irish and English papers, and carried on an extensive correspondence. One of the heaviest pieces of literary investigation work I engaged in was a memorial with tables and evidence annexed showing the flimsey grounds upon which a number of tenants in Crossmaglen were convicted and sent to varying terms of imprisonment. It is interesting now to look over these old papers. The son of one of these men, was deformed or paralyzed. I brought him up to town but Dr McDonnell[104] could do nothing for him. He has ever since been my friend. He is now in the Incurable Hospital.

When writing of Dr McDonnell I should have said that he was by government dismissed from his office of Prison Surgeon on account of his humane treatment of those under his care.

All these years since my cousin Edmund Harvey was working away at his propaganda of leaflets, pamphlets and correspondence, in the cause of Ireland.

Occasionally I attended meetings in England. Many a bloody scene of Police violence did I see here in Ireland, and some of lesser note of a mob and party character.

A bright episode was the viceroyalty of the Aberdeens, after Gladstone had come round to Home Rule.[105] I never expected as then occasionally to meet the Viceregal pair and to be asked to lunch at the Viceregal Lodge. Their Private Secretary Colonel Turner[106] often called upon me at the Printing Office professing warm Home Rule feeling. (After this he turned round and became one of the worst instruments in carrying out Balfour's system of coercion.)[107] In those days Miss Dunn[108] remarked to me: 'Well now, you are reaping the results of your labours.'

But it was not to be. The clouds settled down again upon us. A coercion act, more comprehensive in some respects worse than any of the previous 60 since the Union, was enacted, and was made perpetual, which none of the others were.

I could not always toe the party line, and brought odium upon myself from some of my extreme friends, especially upon two occasions.

Mr Field, a Dublin tradesman was known to have upon a jury acted a peculiarly obnoxious part in convicting some of our friends. An attempt was made to assassinate him. I 'drew the line' of fight at this, and became fellow-Secretary with Lord Ardilaun of a Committee which presented him with an address of condolence, and instituted a collection for him.[109]

The Curtins were a nationalist family living in Kerry. There was a raid for arms on their house. Mr Curtin resisted and was shot. The family gave evidence that led to some of the perpetrators, neighbours of theirs, being put into Penal Servitude. The family were cruelly boycotted and had to be protected by police. I went down to show my sympathy with them and investigate the case. I stopped the night with them and went to Mass with them. After Mass the seat on which we sat was taken out of the church by a party of girls and smashed before our eyes. There was unnecessary violence by the police. I attempted to address the people on behalf of the family. I would not be listened to: and my life would not have been worth much but for the police. I returned to Dublin prepared and determined to give my experiences in full. The *Freeman* begged me to delay my article. Mr Parnell sent over a special messenger to stop me. At length I agreed to meet John Dillon and argue the point with him in the presence of Dr McDonnell and Abraham Shackleton (both of whom thought I should publish) and I agreed to abide by the decision of those two. The meeting came off. After all was said they advised me not to publish. Shortly the argument was, that it would not affect the position of the Curtins, and it would certainly be used as an argument for further coercion. Nothing ever more convinced me of the evil results of the land system and of the system under which Ireland was governed than what I saw at Fi[e]ries on this occasion. The people were a fine handsome, good faced set. The raid for arms was a boyish prank, like boys looking for apples. If he had not opposed them Mr Curtin would not have been shot. Even when shot his family should not have been eager to help in convicting 'the poor harmless young fellows'. The Curtins had to leave the district. I considered it somewhat disingenuous of my nationalist friends who so entirely disapproved of my visit to the Curtins, afterwards, at the Parnell Commission to instance my interference as evidence of the efforts put forward by members of the National League to stop boycotting.

And then English visitors and sympathizers poured over. John Morley, James Bryce, William Morris, Shaw Lefevre, and many others of less note sat and asked questions and sought information, and my views on affairs.[110] Shaw Lefevre I am doubtful of. I spent part of two days with him at Grays and visiting evicted farms. I am doubtful as to his being at the office.

Murrough O'Brien invited me to meet Morley at his lodgings. We had beefsteaks potatoes and much talk. We then sallied out to find a bed for Morley. It was horseshow week, and no bed was to be had. We left Morley to occupy O'Briens bed, and I brought the latter out to Highfield-road. All there were in bed. I made up a shakedown for O'Brien on the parlour floor where he slept comfortably and was off early next morning to look after Morley's breakfast.

The Morley and Ripon Reception early in 1888 was a great affair. The task of editing the proceedings of this as of previous and subsequent Conventions was thrown upon me.

E. D. Gray, Editor of the *Freeman* then kept a fine house and gave entertainments at the visits of English sympathizers.[111] He like Butt was a strange mixture of good and bad. Unlike Butt he was honest in money matters. His wife was a fine woman who sacrificed herself for his reformation. I believe on occasions she had taken him out of houses of ill-fame in London. Politically Gray was a great loss. Had he lived the Split might have been avoided — or at least rendered less keen and fatal. His wife married again and leads a quiet life on an Island in one of the Shannon Lakes.

Many were the delightful excursions with parties of English sympathizers to Glendalough, the Dargle, the Vartry Waterworks and elsewhere. T. D. Sullivan would delight us with his songs, such as 'God Save Ireland' and 'Marty Hynes' — the best song the agitation evolved. At a great Party at V. B. Dillon's[112] we met W. S. Blunt (who had been in prison for us) and his wife, daughter of Byron's Ada.[113] Well do I remember Dr Spence Watson and a party of us entertained by the PP at Loughrea, where we Protestants were hardly allowed to touch some fine fish (it was a Friday) and where I was made to sing 'God Save Ireland'.

And then the excitement at evictions. I carried away a crowbar (which I have still) from one taken from the landlords party; and at one I met a young reporter Henry Norman, now an MP and famous for his books on Russia and China.[114]

And many were the new friends we made: Miss Borthwick, a London Artist, now a Gaelic scholar, resident near us.[115] I first met her at some trials in Tipperary. After that she commenced Irish from primers. We met her with them in London busses.

There was Rose Kavanagh, a sweet beautiful girl, who wrote some nice pieces of poetry.[116]

W. A. MacDonnell [*recte* Macdonald] a cranky blind Clergyman took greatly to us and the cause.[117] His wife he made almost a slave to him. I was several times at his house in London. To enter Parliament he unfrocked himself much against my advice. He was not a success there and it soured him. We have never seen anything of him since the Parnell Split. They lived latterly at Killiney where his poor wife died.

And Henry George was at our house and discussed his theories with persons we asked to meet him.[118]

By far the pleasantest friendship we made was with Charlotte G. O'Brien,[119] daughter of William S. O'Brien and her sister-in-law Mrs Dickson. We were more than once on holidays with Miss O'Brien at Foynes and she was often with us. And Mrs Dickson and her daughter spent several days once at Highfield-road. Miss O'Brien was charming and enthusiastic. She wrote some good poetry about the League and the movement. She had interested herself much in the condition of girl emigrants, and had even gone third class to America to see for herself the real state of affairs on the passage. In the middle of our intercourse with her she became, much to the astonishment of us all, a Catholic. She was deaf. I learned the manual alphabet so as to be able to speak to her. It was charming at her place at Foynes. Gardening and rearing Irish terriers were some of her tastes. The dogs would sometimes fall out and have frightful fights under the table which she would not hear. After the Split we saw little of her. She took up Mr Parnell's side warmly. I believe the raising of Daffodils is now one of her occupations. She has singularly little veneration or love of the past, and I think easily took up and laid down friendships. When in Tasmania I went to much trouble to procure drawings of and relics from the different houses her father had inhabited. On my return she appeared scarcely to care for or regard them.

A distinctly new phase of my life now opens. I give up business and enter Parliament, the last move the natural outcome of my devotion for so many years to Irish politics.

I give up Business and Enter Parliament

My attention to public affairs and the drawing away of customers on account of the opinions I so openly expressed had had a correspondingly depressing effect upon my business. After making up my books on 1st January 1890 I decided upon retiring. The possibility of my doing so was not mainly due to my own exertions. It was mainly due to a series of untoward events. Had Father and Mother lived to a normal age, had Annie and Richard lived, or if they had lived but a few years more and left children the means which had come to be centred in the hands of my sister and myself would have been happily divided. Trusting alone to the means and savings we ourselves would have been able to make, it is scarcely likely we would ever have travelled far out of the United Kingdom or that I would have ever entered Parliament. I enjoyed the fruits of the toils and savings of others. We might have been able to retire. Business was ever such a grind that I would have been most anxious to obtain relief from it, even if we had had to live in an humble way.

We had taken a young man into our house and I had been training him to the business. I now took him into partnership, reserving to myself an annual fixed tribute. He had good abilities and might have prospered, and I might have had the old place as a foothold in Dublin. And it would always have been a pleasure to me to be able to dabble a little amongst the type (Even the smell of a Printing office is grateful to me to this day.) The arrangement however did not prove satisfactory. In how few simple words one may sum up the recollections of months of grinding anxiety! I sold the business to Thom and Co.[120] I was reconciled to the loss as compared to what it stood in books, by my staff of effective workpeople being taken on into the new employ. We dissolved partnership on 28th October, 1893, and the business commenced at 10 William-street by my Father on or about 10th December 1828, came to an end. It had on the whole served us well. Thom & Co kept on my premises for a few months. I then sold them to a next door neighbour. The plant of my office was brought across to Thom's. It there perished in a fire a few years afterwards. What I most regretted was the desk at which Robert Chapman and Father, and Richard and I had so long worked. The only relics I possess of my Printing office life and Father's, besides a few old account books, are: – part of the shelving of Father's book shop, including the press in which the Sheares head[s] used to be preserved: a piece of iron which I use for a door weight and which belonged to Brunswick-street, and some printers 'sticks' and measuring-rule. My devoted foreman, Peter Lawler, had saved a few hundred pounds. I added £100 to it, and allowed him a small pension. He was quite too delicate to offer any hope of his obtaining other employ. I shall write of him again farther on.

When I retired from business my plans of life were somewhat indefinite. They naturally turned to more entire devotion to the cause of Home Rule. I put myself at the disposal of Mr Parnell. On the 24th Feb. 1890, whilst on a political mission to England on the invitation of our friends Mr & Mrs Byles in Bradford, and the Countess Russell at Richmond,[121] I received a telegram informing me that I had, without opposition been elected member for West Waterford. I may say once for all that I received nothing but kindness and consideration from the constituency. They again elected me without opposition or expense in 1892 and 1895. The devotion and consideration shown by Irish constituencies to their MPs is to this day a puzzle and a subject of envy to Members on the other side of the channel. I was warmly received whenever I went down to address them. The first occasion, a few months after my election was a peculiarly and somewhat enthusiastically brilliant one. Lizzie and some of the Harvey girls and Edmund came with me. The embarrassment of the old PP at having to entertain ladies was apparent.

Patrick J. Power, my colleague in the representation of the county and still in Parliament, I found to be an admirable man.[122] He and I became fast friends.

That first season in Parliament was in truth a golden, never to be forgotten time. The Conservatives were in power, but the whole trend of feeling in Gt Britain was in our favour; and success within a few years appeared certain. We Irish were, in and out of Parliament, the 'white headed boys'. Grand entertainments were given in our favour, and no Liberal election or public meeting was complete without the presence of some of us — even I with my feeble powers of platform speaking was often called upon to bear a part. In Parliament I at once felt at home. Already I knew personally nearly all of our Party and very many of the English and Scotch members. Our unity and brotherhood were the envy of other parties. If a prince and princess were being married there could scarcely have been greater doings than we had at the marriage of William O'Brien.[123] The past and the present met in brilliant gatherings on The Terrace — collateral descendants of Robert Emmet's (direct of Thomas Addis Emmet) met there old Repealers like the O'Gorman Mahon[124] and young recruits to the cause of Ireland such as Sir Thomas Esmonde and Vesey Knox.[125] (Kathleen Emmet broke the hearts of all the young men of our party, and gave me her portrait.) We did not see much of our Leader; when we did, he was, so much as it was reasonable to expect of a man so much above us to be, friendly, helpful and gracious. Often in those months I felt the cup of my happiness overflowing. To think that in my time the cause of Ireland was about to succeed and that I was being permitted to take a part in it!

[Webb devotes 200 words here to describing a family called Pelly, whom he and his wife met on a train journey.]

Our Parliamentary Party then numbered 87. 24 are still in Parliament, 2 of these gone over to the government, at least not in the Party. 31 are dead, — 15 of them suddenly! 34 have retired or have not been reelected. There is some discrepancy here — 24 + 31 + 34 = 89. I understood it when making up the figures. I do not care to go to the trouble of clearing up the ambiguity.

The latter part of the session Lizzie was at home. I spent all my spare time with Madame Venturi — gradually coming to lunch with her before I went down to the house. She was a most interesting woman, a confirmed smoker. She had known all the Italian patriots and was specially attached to Mazzini. We were engaged preparing his letters for the press. When the session was over we laid aside the work intending to resume it on my return to London. It was never taken up again. The Split came. I think it broke her heart. She never could understand how it was that I and others did not adhere to Mr Parnell. She died soon afterwards. I was the only anti Parnellite at her funeral. She however bore with John Dillon. She had some idea that Mazzini's spirit had passed into him, and she bequeathed to him most of her library of Italian books.

[The next 800 words describe visits the Webbs made to Scotland with members of the family. Because they could not afford to keep up two houses while Alfred Webb was in London, they gave up their Dublin house and moved in to live with his sister Deborah.]

The Parnell Split

I would gladly draw a veil over this episode in Irish history, and my life. Mr Parnell had for some time been living with the wife of Captain O'Shea[126] — he married her immediately after the divorce proceedings. The question was whether, considering all the circumstances of the case as known on the morning of 26th November (1890), including the impression he had given those who suspected something was wrong, as to what the outcome of the trial would be. Considering our duty towards Ireland, Mr Parnell, ourselves, Mr Gladstone and the Liberal Party and the friends in England who had come out on our side, was it, or was it not desirable that Mr Parnell should for the present continue our Leader? After wearying and heartbreaking debates, in Room No. 15, House of Commons, at 5.12 on the afternoon on 6th December, we divided, 33, including proxies standing by Mr Parnell; 53 of us, including proxies, retiring and electing Justin McCarthy chairman.[127] We who from the first viewed Mr Parnell's conduct in a fatally unfavourable light certainly put ourselves in the wrong when, not fully informed, we condoned his conduct on the 20th in Dublin at a meeting at the Leinster Hall, and on the 25th in London by reelecting him chairman. I am still of opinion that having gone wrong, it was better for us to retrace our steps at the last moment, than for the sake of consistency adhere to our decision of the 25th.

In coming to decision on one side and the other, I could trace no motive but a sincere desire in all, except perhaps one case, to do what was right. I shall not attempt to specify the blame in that case, because I should have to specify and detail it in another, and I have now no desire to do that. Most of my nationalist relatives and friends, better people than I, held by Mr Parnell. But for the sympathy and approval of my Wife and Sister I do not know how I could have lived through those times. The note in my diary on the day after I heard the verdict (I was then worn out giving up Lisnabin) is: 'Sore, physically, mentally, morally.' The Irish Protestant Home Rule Association, after a close debate in which I took part decided overwhelmingly in Mr Parnell's favour, and I resigned my Vice Presidency. Dublin was overwhelmingly in his favour. I doubt if ever there was a scene of greater enthusiasm than when shortly after this Mr Parnell was received in the Rotunda; or of deeper more sincere mourning than when a year later his remains were consigned to Glassnevin [*sic*]. In the House of Commons, we who a few days before called each other by our Christian-names, now passed without recognizing each other. Shocking scenes of violence occurred at elections and gatherings in Ireland. Lime was thrown in Mr Parnell's face: he was nearly blinded. Others of his side were injured. On our side two at least narrowly escaped with their lives. Nothing but my comparative insignificance saved me upon one occasion.

We had to differ. But all this should not have been. It was however inevitable. The English who held up their hands in horror at us, and drew away from our cause in consequence of our actions, would under the same circumstances have borne themselves no more wisely. As well ask famishing wretches on a raft at sea to bear themselves with calmness and act with forbearance, when they see certain relief disappear, through their own differences as to the conduct of their chief.

A few days before and Home Rule appeared near and certain. Fourteen years have passed and there are no signs of its accomplishment. The full magnitude of the disaster was not realized by any of us at the time. I remember Barry O'Brien[128], the well known author, saying to me in the Lobby of the House of Commons, in the days after the split, 'Home Rule is now deferred for ten years.' We must not however be too certain that even if the Split had not occurred, if there had been no Divorce case, and if Mr Parnell had lived, Home Rule would have been of as easy or proximate accomplishment as we then believed.

[*The following 950 words describe the life that Alfred and Elizabeth Webb led while he was in parliament, when they lived in both London and Dublin, and their day-to-day life.*]

I spent much of my time when in the House reading and writing in the Library, where I soon came to have a table of my own looking out on the Thames. Lizzie was often in the Ladies Gallery, or in Summer with me on the Terrace. She came to know the members and the proceedings in the Chamber as well as I did myself. She was fonder of listening to speeches than I; so that she often knew more of what went on.

I took my full share of questioning and occasionally spoke briefly, sometimes I am sure making a fool of myself. I never effected anything or made my mark in any legislation. The most insignificant member on a public board has more direct influence over public affairs than has an ordinary member in Parliament. The most important part I ever took was in proposing a motion on the opium traffic. My speech on this occasion was printed and widely circulated. Mr Gladstone and Mr Morley said kind things of me — the one, generally, was urged more by kindly feeling than on much basis of truth — the other commendation was in regard to a certain speech of mine on Irish affairs, and was perhaps partly merited. I am now amazed at the way I then obliged myself against my natural inclination to do my best at speaking. On the subject of Home Rule, during the passage of the Bill — the object that brought me into Parliament — I never uttered a word. There were plenty of good speakers, and as it was the policy of the opposition to smother the debate with verbiage it was the cue of our rank and file to keep silence. I never missed a division on the Home Rule Question. Indeed during my sojourn in the House there were few more regular attenders, and I never paired but once.

It is no small satisfaction to look back upon intercourse with such men as Gladstone,[129] Morley, Bradlaugh[130] — to remember pleasant talks in the Tea Room with Labouchere[131] and Sir W. Lawson.[132] Outside the House we were invited to many a brilliant gathering. I was often sent, much against my grain, to speak at public meetings in distant parts of England and help at elections. We paid an interesting visit to Henry J. Wilson at Sheffield, and there at a meeting on the upper floor of a large factory Lizzie acquitted herself creditably in a short extempore speech.

One election campaign I went through in the dead of winter, in what district I have forgotten, the roads deep in snow. An evening with the keeper of an old wooden windmill whirring and creaking in the blast comes back to me; and I think of his wife's delicious hot cakes and strong, rich tea.

My most congenial work was with Henry J. Wilson and men of that class on humanitarian questions such as opium, C[ontagious] D[iseases] discussions and the colour problem. I joined in giving a breakfast to Miss Wells, a coloured lady, who had come over to enlist our sympathies against lynching, and another to two fine American women who had exerted themselves in combatting the vice regulation system in India.[133]

My locker on the Lobby, where I kept my books and papers was No. 262.

A special case I took up of which I still retain the papers, and in which I may have had some influence, was the brutal treatment by the captain of the crew of the *Port Yarrock*, and her subsequent wreck with all hands on the coast of Ireland in 1894.[134]

On one of our pleasant Sunday rambles near London — that day in Windsor park — we met and spent most of an afternoon with a peculiarly intelligent artizan and his daughter and gave them tea in the garden of a hotel. We made a great mistake in not keeping their address and seeing more of them — 'Ships that pass in the night'.

We entertained numbers of our friends and relatives at different times in London.

In intervals, such as Easter holidays we took lodgings and had pleasant times by the sea at Felixstowe, Lowestoft, Hastings and Charmouth, and inland at Gomshall in Surrey, where we enjoyed a visit from Annie Waring. At Lyme Regis by Charmouth we trod the pier whereon one of Miss Austen's Heroines sprained her foot; and there we were entertained at tea by a friendly coast-guard officer and his daughter.

One of the most interesting old time characters I became acquainted with in London was one of my fellow Irish members, the O'Gorman Mahon. He had fought duels in his time and had been one of the proposers of O'Connell at the Clare election. He belonged to an old Irish family and had lived much of his life in France where he had imbibed any but very orthodox Catholic opinions. When we knew him most he was confined to his room or to his bed and was near his end. He never could understand our teetotalism. 'Well, if you are afraid of the wine, I have here some whiskey I can recommend.' I took my nephew Willy W. Shackleton, then a medical student to see him. When leaving he exclaimed to me in a stage whisper: 'Handsome young fellow d—d handsome.' Talking freely on religious topics, he said to me of certain beliefs: 'Of course we believe them, the Priests say they are true; but between you and me they are all d—d nonsense.' After his death, some lady cousins in Ireland, knowing I had been with him much at the last, were anxious to find out from me whether he had died a good Catholic. I necessarily avoided meeting them. There was something pathetic in his childlike life and loneliness in a narrow London lodgings, and in a certain sense in his innocence — he must have been about 90 years of age, when one thought of the stirring life he had once led. His landlady carefully tended him, he much depended on her. She gave me his silver spectacles. I was one of those who accompanied his remains from London to Glasnevin.

Besides our Cousins Lydia Maria and Dr Helen Webb the following were those with whom we became most intimate, and at whose houses we were most sure of a welcome.

Charles Schwann, MP and his wife.[135] They were wealthy and kept a fine house in Princes Gardens. She was one of the Duncan girls.[136] It was a great change for her since the days I remembered her a little girl playing about the strand at Greystones in a plaid frock. Their sons were at one of the English public schools. Their little daughter used to dance beautifully for our amusement.

Mrs Duncan and her unmarried daughters lived at Hammersmith, the house full, the walls covered with beautiful engravings collected by her husband. The little garden stretched down pleasantly to the Thames. When last we visited London together in 1899 they were living at Richmond. Mrs Duncan has since died, leaving Janie (the most attractive of all the girls) and Emily living we presume together.

J. F. X. O'Brien, one of my MP colleagues, a sterling character, had been condemned to be hung, drawn and quartered, and had suffered a long term of imprisonment in Fenian times.[137] He was and is one of the honestest and most conscientious men I have ever known. His wife a simple honest Cork woman. A numerous second family of boys and girls, on small means, with the strictest economy they have since managed to bring them up and start them in life. The eldest girl Annie, is with her Father in the London office of the Irish Party. One of the Boys is a Doctor in fair practice. One girl is a schoolmistress, and another is completing her musical education in Munich — she sent me some 'Fliegende' [light songs] the other day. These two last girls when young used to delight us with Spanish dances, taught them by an elderly nun in a Convent! By a previous marriage J.F.X. had two sons who are priests. These young people spoke French and German.

We became intimate with Alfred Marks, a retired banker, who with his wife, the authoress of several novels, and four children live in South Hampstead.[138] Admirable, liberal minded people, deeply interested in Irish affairs. We took many pleasant excursions together — to some of the Cinque Ports, to hear nightingales, which I am not sure whether we heard or not; and he and I by ourselves took some ever to be remembered walks in Surrey. He was full of all sorts of curious knowledge about the topography of the country round London. The girls have become musicians. One son is an engineer in the North of England — another an artist in Paris. I shall later have occasion to refer to the Markses as opponents of the Transvaal War.

Lady Agatha Russell, daughter of Lord John Russell was one of the visitors to Ireland during the coercion regime.[139] We then became acquainted with her. Later I had stopped at her mother, the Countess Russell's, house in Richmond Park, Pembroke Lodge, a rambling old place, beautifully situated, lent them by the Queen. They were liberal, both in religion and politics. There we were always welcome and lunched occasionally on Sundays. They lived in the simplest style, in the midst of books, Russell portraits and memorials of the days when Lord John used to be Prime Minister. Some of the People we met there spoke casually of the Queen and court circles and functions as part of their lives. Once in Lizzie's absence I spent a day, & I believe a night, with them at a mansion they had hired at Hindhead. The Countess had been intimate with Moore, and played his melodies with a sweet touch.[140] In Spring the snowdrops and bluebells covered the ground under the trees round Pembroke Lodge. The Countess is now dead and Lady Agatha and her brother have both built houses at Haslemere. We still correspond.

It was always pleasant to meet our cousin Charles Waring. He was employed at Edmondson's in Westminster. He was a thoughtful beautiful character, whom I had first seen as a chubby little boy at Ballinclay. The illness was at this time coming on, which, after a voyage to Australia, in the vain search of health, carried him off a few years after the time I am now writing of. He is one of the many quiet spirits I have known who made little stir in the world, and whose removal closely affected but few; and who yet are remembered with deep affection by those who knew them.

In a review, we read by chance one day a notice of *The Journal of Emily Shore*.[141] We bought the book, were delighted with it, and spent a couple of days tracing up the localities where she had lived, and which she described, on the confines of Bedford and Cambridge-shires. We wrote to the unknown authoress through the publisher, and had an immediate reply from one of Emily Shore's two surviving sisters, Louisa and Arabella. They knew me well by repute, were ardent Home Rulers. That was the commencement of the closest friendship we made in London. They had a beautiful place, Orchard Poyle, a couple of miles from Taplow Station, in the midst of typical lovely English scenery, woods, heaths, winding roads and lanes shaded by trees. There we spent many afternoons sitting in the garden or indoors amongst books and old surroundings. Occasionally we spent the night there. The sisters were, when we first became acquainted with them, from 60 to 65 years of age. They were deeply learned, translating from the Greek and Italian, interested in all liberal movements, and in religious thought, the very pink of Womanhood. They kept a somewhat stately coachman in a neat two storied lodge near by, and complained that as soon as they had put him in the way of owning it, he had become a conservative and thus voted, whilst they had of course no vote to maintain their opinions. A superannuated horse dreamed out his life in their paddock, and trotted up for apples. Even the toads in their garden were befriended. Thence we started on little excursions, exploring Milton's and William Penn's country, to Beaconsfield, to Windsor, and to see the church in the graveyard of which Gray wrote his Elegy, and where he was buried. The sisters had written several volumes of poetry. They like the Russells had been brought up in Orthodoxy.

Autumn of 1891 to the Autumn of 1894

When the House broke up in the Autumn of 1891 we spent some weeks at Port Bannatyne with Hannah E. White.[142] That winter we were some weeks with her in Cork and our time in Dublin was spent between Deborahs and Anna Liffey.[143] I wrote letters and articles for the *N.Y. Nation* and *Manchester Guardian*. The business anxieties which soon afterwards compelled me to sell the printing office were then heavy on me. In February 1892 Parliament reopened and we returned to London. In the summer the Government dissolved and I had a busy time of it electioneering in England and at home. I was returned unopposed for West Waterford. The Liberals came in with a majority of 40 counting us as voting with them. The Irish Party stood: 9 Parnellites under the chairmanship of John Redmond, and 72 of our men under Justin McCarthy.

We were becoming more and more attached to our cousin Hannah E. White. Though but 14 years separated from us in age, the relationship between her and us had become more like that between parent and grown up children then between cousins. Cork had become a second home. I felt that in any attention I could pay her I was in some measure vicariously repaying what I owed my parents.

Parliament met and on 11th August the conservatives were formally defeated. A week afterwards Lizzie, Hannah, her companion Mary

Looney and I started via the Rhine for a tour on the Continent and in Switzerland. We spent a month delightfully wandering about together. Then Lizzie and I saw them off home in a sleeping car for Calais at Bâle. Next day our niece Mary E. Shackleton joined us. We walked over the St Gotthard Pass into Italy, visited Miss Dunn in Florence, — having been some weeks on Lago Maggiore and at Venice — and passing through Perugia, settled down in Rome early in November. There we remained two months. Mary was pleasant company and up to everything. She made friends wherever we went. Lilly Green (now Mrs Reeves) and Mary Hayden[144] joined us for a time — the one a Quaker and like a Catholic — the other a Catholic and Quaker-like in manner. Their company added much to the interest of our stay. Passing through Paris in terribly severe weather, we reached home. The death of Huldah B. Harvey, Newenham's wife saddened us soon after our arrival in Dublin.

The session of 1893 was almost entirely devoted to the attempt to pass a Home Rule Bill. It was a most interesting and exciting season. I cannot here attempt to journalize it in particulars. It was introduced on the 13th February and passed on 1st September. There were 195 divisions in all of which I voted. It was carried by only 34 votes; and was killed in the Lords on 8th September by 419 votes to 41. The savage shouts with which this last result was received by the mob, collected in the Palace Yard, were a striking contrast to the apparent enthusiasm for Home Rule in England a few years before. As they rang in my ears I felt that my Parliamentary Life was drawing to a close. An illness of some days in London succeeded, then weeks of harassing negotiations in Dublin relative to the disposal of my business. There was a short Autumn session. We spent Christmas in Cork with Hannah White. Then to London for a while and back to Cork again.

We were now in 1894. That year brought us the loss of many friends — Alexander Ireland,[145] John Edmondson, O'Neill Daunt, an old Repeal friend, a coadjutor of O'Connell's, John F. Waller an Irish Poet,[146] Samuel Mumford of Detroit, our Cousin Thomas Waring of Ferns. Frederick Douglass who had a few years previously visited us to renew old memories of the 40's at Brunswick-street, died aged 78 about this time. His career had indeed been a remarkable one — fresh from slavery when we first knew him, a man of considerable eminence in the US when he died.

The session of 1894 was a most thankless and harassing one — we were engaged helping the government to pass bills in which we had little real interest. Gladstone resigned on 3rd March, and with him disappeared all present hope of Home Rule. His last speech, and quiet retirement behind the Speakers chair was one of the most dramatic scenes that ever passed before my eyes. I began to count the days until I would be free from Parliament.

On 10th of November I was astonished to receive a telegram from my friend Dadabhai Naoroji, a Parsee colleague of mine in Parliament asking if I was prepared to sail on the 22nd for Bombay to act as President of the Indian National Congress — all expenses paid! After a few words with Lizzie I telegraphed acceptance. It must have been my attitude in Parliament towards Indian questions that led to this most flattering proposal being made. Until the day of sailing my time, in Dublin, was fully occupied working up Indian affairs at the libraries and arranging for a proper wardrobe; and in London in interviews with friends of the congress.

My time during the earlier portion of the passage was fully occupied in the preparation of my address, which was put in type immediately on my landing at Bombay and which with the other addresses I delivered in India is still on sale.

I had a deeply interesting voyage of 24 days to Bombay — in the *Ballarat* P and O as far as Aden, then transferring into the *Clyde*. The weather was finer than when I had before been in the Mediterranean. We saw much of the African coast, and spent a day at Malta. The passage through the Canal and Red Sea was deeply interesting. Aden in the Steam Launch that came out to meet me & in the carriage placed at my disposal on shore I had some premonition of the princely style in which I was received at Bombay. Mr Wacha, a Parsee gentleman, was foremost amongst those that met me on landing. He is one of the foremost Indian reformers, and was my guide, philosopher, and friend during my stay.

He since visited us in Dublin, we were invited to his daughter's wedding, as we have been invited to other family functions in India, and we have kept up a correspondence. Wacha and I left for Madras at 9 p.m. on the 20th December and reached at 8 on the morning of the 22nd. Occasionally at Stations we were roused up in the night and I in my pyjamas had to receive addresses and listen to bands of music. An immense crowd met me at Madras, and I had to receive addresses and make speeches. Then in a carriage with men running before to clear the way I was brought to a mansion specially reserved for me in centre of a fine park. Mr Wacha and other celebrities lodged in the same house; but the theory was that they were my guests. I sat at the head of the table. A body guard of some 100 young men attended me when I went out — a band of music preceded me in my progresses to and from the Congress held in a 'pandal' [arbour] near by a state umbrella held over me. Drives, visits of ceremony to distinguished persons, receptions at temples, entertainments in my honour, garlandings, fireworks, photographings, fully occupied my time before and after the meetings of the Congress.

The Congress lasted four days. It was held in a 'pandal' or hall, specially erected for the occasion, with sides open above a certain height, and inside beautifully hung with white drapery. There were 1160 delegates and perhaps 2000 visitors. They presented a gorgeous sight, all but a few on the platform in every variety of eastern costume and headdress — the colours blending harmoniously like a bed of tulips. England has ruled India primarily for her own advantage alone — she has, however conferred upon her one inestimable blessing, a common language — English. All but a few speeches were in that language — those in Indian tongues were translated for me. My Address was well received. I had no difficulty in conducting the proceedings. I surprised myself. It showed me what one can do if one is put to it. But for the nerve I was able to show, and the personal authority I asserted upon one occasion, there would have been a serious break up. I had to refuse a resolution which the only English lady delegate present wanted to put. She had many adherents present and for a few minutes on the first day it was all but 'touch and go'.[147] She was closely connected in the philanthropic circles I was most intimate with in London. She sent home dreadful reports of my action, and it was some time after my return until I was able to persuade my friends of the reasonableness of my action. The delicate attention with which I was received and treated all through passes belief. In a few years after my death there is scarcely any likelihood of any trace of my existence being left on the face of Irish affairs. As President of the Tenth Indian National Congress it is likely to stand for sometime on the Native Records of India. After ten years I occasionally receive tokens of remembrance that surprise me. The Records of the Congress are to be found in all important collections of books relating to Indian affairs. The delegates were of all religions from Christian to members of a small caste where the rule is for brothers to have a wife in common. The vast proportion were Hindoos of different castes; a proportion, numbering amongst them some of the most important members, were Mohammedans. These last in India take up somewhat that position that Protestants do in Ireland. Originally intruders most of them fear that as the mass of their fellow countrymen obtain rights their position in the country will become less secure. There have now (1905) been 20 Congresses. But three Presidents I believe have been other than Hindu, Mahommedan or Parsee.

The mental strain had been severe. I was not sorry when I found myself alone with a native servant visiting places of interest in the north of India — more especially Delhi and Agra. The remains of ancient civilizations, and the fortresses and palaces of the Middle ages were interesting beyond anything I could have imagined. The Taj at Agra is indeed the loveliest building in the world according to the ideals of the Arabian Nights. I saw it thrice in shine, in thunder storm, and by moon light, and did not know under which aspect to admire it most. At Baroda I spend a couple of days with an old young friend Mr Littledale. A few, perhaps 10 years before, he a lad had come to bid me good bye in the Printing Office. He since had resided in India; had married a native girl and lost her, and was now married to an English lady. He had become a mighty hunter of wild beasts (20000 people annually are killed by them and snakes in India).

I spent a few days pleasantly with Ernest and Zaide Munnings at Itarsi — two nights of which were with Ernest in tents in the Jungle, where his missionary work called him. A tiger had lately carried off cattle in the vicinity. What we saw of a primitive race the Ghonds was specially interesting — Indeed all those weeks were crammed with interest. No one that has not seen India knows what the world really is.

I reached Bombay at 7 a.m. on the 16th satiated and worn out with travelling and experiences. It was Wednesday. I was to sail on Saturday, and I hoped for rest, and time to collect my thoughts, and enjoy a little social intercourse with my Indian friends. This was not to be. The Theatre in Bombay had been taken for the following, Thursday, evening and I, who felt as if I had not a spare idea in my head was expected to give an address, and justify the reports Bombay had heard of my conduct of the Congress. Never in my many experiences had I so completely felt myself to be 'Between the Devil and the deep sea'.

That evening, getting clear of my friends I shut myself up in my room with candles, pens, ink and paper, and set to work. I had scarcely got into my work before I felt exhausted and went to bed. At 2 in the morning, I woke, lit the candles, tied a wet towel round my head and resumed. Before long thought began to flow. I finished and had time for a rest before a late breakfast and Mr Wacha appeared. The address satisfied him even better than my Presidential one. It was put in type at once and I delivered it to a crowded and enthusiastic audience.

Next day, Friday, was devoted to an excursion by special steamer to Alibagh on the other side of the bay — a passage of an hour or two. A crowd with musical instruments met us on the palm-fringed beach, and I in a palanquin on mens' shoulders was photographed with the crowd and the musicians. I had to deliver another address at a village a mile or so inland. There was a banquet (the cocoanuts brought down fresh from the trees) and a number of women danced and sang for me. A reception in my honour at the House of Mr Tata a wealthy Parsee brought the day to a conclusion.[148] It was pleasant at this party to see numbers of Parsee ladies in their graceful dress. The seclusion of women in Hindu society strikes us as painful though they themselves cling most closely to it. The chief of my guard in Madras brought me to see his little brothers and sisters, largely naked unless where covered with chains and trinkets. His mother and aunt would regard me only through the chink of a door. A wealthy Hindu lady went so far as to be present at an entertainment her sons gave in my honour at Madras. I was warned by Mr Wacha not to go too near her and on no account to offer my hand. I forgot — after the Tata soiree I drove out to the government house in compliance with an invitation and dined with Lord Harris, governor of Bombay and his family.[149]

I left, again in *The Clyde*, next day — my cabin being filled by my friends with fruit and flowers.

It would not be easy to enumerate the many beautiful Indian characters with whom I became acquainted, the names of most of whom I have forgotten. The extreme poverty of the mass of the people impressed me. (The brilliant climate there, cloaks indigence as our damp climate accentuates and adds horrors to it.) Our average income in these countries is £40 per individual per annum. There it is 25/– to 30/–. Upon the whole I believe the lives of the Indian people to be more really Christian than ours.

The day after sailing a smart attack of jungle fever developed. I had three further accessions of it — in London, at Deborahs, and on the voyage to Australia. An Irish Doctor, a young fellow, saw me through on the *Clyde*. Some years afterwards, clinging on to the back of a crowded tram in Rathmines I found a young man next me strikingly like my *Clyde* friend. 'Had you a brother in the P and O service', I asked? 'Yes,' he replied, 'are you Mr Webb; my brother told me of you.'

At Aden we transhipped into the *Mussilia*. I disembarked at Brindisi. Except in the Campagna round Rome the weather was bitterly cold the whole way to London and in London. I spent a day in Rome with Miss Tolerton and Miss Creeth, and one in Florence with the Dunns. That was the last I saw of Miss Dunn, one of the closest friends I ever made out of my immediate circle. 'Of such is the Kingdom of God.'

In London I had to rise from sick bed in a private hospital and drive (in a carriage provided for me by my cousins) to a breakfast given in my honour at the National Liberal Club. There were many prominent in Indian circles, amongst others, Sir William Hunter, the Historian of India.[150] Many there were also of my Irish colleagues included in the invitation. That charming man, the author of several books of biography and reminiscence sat next me, George Russell, cousin of our friends the Russells of Pembroke Lodge.[151]

I found Lizzie safe at Hannah White's in Cork where she had spent the weeks of my absence.

Last months in Parliament

We returned to London in March (1895) and, Mr Burrowes being occupied we had for a time to put up near at 4 Alfred Place. We had the Suliots, the Anna Liffey boys, and many other visitors that season. It was a dull hopeless time in Parliament. Socially Arabella Shore's death threw a gloom over our life – she had lived long enough to enjoy my Indian letters. The English were getting tired of the Home rule Question. Our people at Home were growing hopeless and apathetic. When I entered Parliament we had but to face the Conservatives. Now also we were at variance with the Parnellite Party, and our own Party was distracted by the machinations of T. M. Healy (a few years before my closest political friend) and a small party of followers, who can have had no other object in view but to bring the movement for Home Rule to an end. I have known many extraordinary mental changes in my time – none more so than his. He had for years been the very embodiment of the agitation. He was now reported to have said that 'we were only chasing moonbeams'. Like a school boy I counted the days until I should be set free.

The end came at last on 21 June. I was down on the Terrace one of a party taking tea with Lady Esmonde. The division bell rang. We went up stairs and the Liberals were defeated. We packed up and returned to Dublin, determining never to be seen in Parliament again. I was caught in the toils and excitement of the Election campaign, was over persuaded, and a third time, while down in fever at my sisters, was returned unopposed Member for West Waterford. This was on the clear understanding that I was to be allowed to carry out our intention of making a tour round the world, and leaving me free on my return to act according to my inclinations. Indeed I believe our berths were already taken to sail in the *Damascus* for Melbourne, on 30th August. I returned to London the middle of August with other members of the Party to arrange a plan of campaign. (The Conservatives had come in with an overwhelming majority. We were on the eve of untold evils and miseries to be worked by them.) It was of first importance that Mr Healy's influence over our councils should be crushed. There was a meeting of our Party on the subject, and a division, the results of which I considered so certain as against him that I did not even wait to hear the numbers announced. I left London next morning only hearing the news, so far as I remember on my arrival in Dublin. Healy's influence, and the fear of his tongue had prevailed: a majority condoned his speeches and action. (No good came of the movement until six years later, when, by deliberate vote of a Convention in Dublin he was expelled from the Party.)

Utterly disgusted and properly convinced of the uselessness of any further sacrifice of myself in Parliament, I from Anna Liffey on 2nd of August resigned my recently conferred seat.

For a few years at times a certain feeling of 'come down' would cross my mind at being no longer an MP. The Boer War finally cleared these away. Parliament from being the Mother of Free nations had become their Murderer. I might almost at anytime within the past ten years as at present reenter Parliament. I trust I shall never again see the inside of the House, unless sentiment in England changes in an unexpected manner – unless the present situation of force, fraud and brutal imperialism is brought to an end. The very word Parliament is in my thoughts connected with almost fruitless strivings and disappointed hopes.

[*The final 8,000 words describe Webb's life in Ireland after he left parliament. He and his wife travelled to Tasmania and the western seaboard of the United States in late 1895. He goes on to assess the state of politics in 1900 and his work as treasurer of the Irish Federation.*]

31st May 1906

The Parnell Split

In the written recollections of my life I purposely passed over lightly the differences that arose in the ranks of Mr Parnell's followers, and in the Irish world at home and abroad, concerning his conduct, as revealed in Divorce proceedings and in Room No. 15 in the House of Commons. These Recollections of mine were intended for a circle of intimate relatives and friends, many of whom had widely and passionately differed from me concerning Mr Parnell. I did not wish to give these last pain; and I did not wish to reawaken bitter recollections and differences.

Feeling as strongly and clearly as ever on the subject, it is right that I should, in separate form from my Recollections, give my view of the questions at issue in 1890. I shall do so shortly. Those who desire to probe the subject must consult the daily press and current literature of the time. Doubtless *The Story of the Parnell Crisis, Pall Mall Gazette Extra, January 1891* will be preserved in some public libraries. Mr Morley's *Life of Gladstone* enters fully into the subject.[152] I shall treat it as it affected myself. Some of those — whom I then most strongly opposed, I am now working with in hearty accord; and, like John Redmond, under. Nothing could be gained by renewing bitter memories. But one owes something to history and to their personal character.

I write under the shadow of the death of Michael Davitt, who viewed the Parnell episode in the same light as I did. He passed away but a few hours ago. Just before his removal to hospital for operation I had at his house two interviews with him on the education questions, to discuss letters which we had from Mr Dillon and Mr Redmond, dissuading us from publicly giving utterance to our views on the subject, and showing how their attitude and that of the Party was not at all the extreme Catholic one it was represented to be by the *Freeman*.

4th June 1906

I was one of those who saw Davitt's remains consigned to Mother earth at Strade on Saturday.[153] His loss is irremediable. I shall now proceed, not deeming it necessary to date my narrative.

I entered Parliament the Spring of 1890 — and that Summer and Autumn were (apart from social bereavements) the happiest and proudest of my life. There was much I could not understand in Mr Parnell's neglect of his Parliamentary duties. I, however, felt persuaded there was some good and sufficient and deep reason therefor. I would, as the saying is, 'have let every drop of blood in my veins have been pumped out for his benefit'. Reports as to some dishonourable liaison with Mrs O'Shea were set at rest by his assurance to Mr Davitt, that if the matter came into court, he would emerge triumphantly. Others, from what I afterwards heard, knew more than I did, and feared more.

When Parliament rose, Lizzie and I returned home and set about breaking up our beautiful home, Lisnabin, on this road; in the assurance that when we settled down again it would be in a Home Ruled Ireland.

Saturday 15th November — We had all but completed when in the evening's papers appeared the horrifying report of the first days trial of the undefended case of O'Shea v. Parnell. Which if it had appeared a week earlier I would most probably have abandoned public life. It would be difficult to describe my anguish. 'Sore physically, mentally, morally.' 'Wringings of heart.' Such are the notes that appear in my diary. What amazed & puzzled me was that the Harveys, Miss O'Brien, Thomas H. and most of my personal friends saw no reason to have less regard for Parnell as a leader. Lizzie and Deborah felt as I did. There was strong condemnation on the part of many of my Parliamentary associates; but the general feeling and report was that if we stood by Parnell he was prepared to explain or justify. As we afterwards realized these reports were craftily put in circulation by his intimate entourage so as to lead us on until it was too late for us to retreat.

We were in the position of the crew of a vessel who after enduring the wrecking storms and buffettings of an apparently endless voyage, thought they were entering a sunny peaceful port. The Captain had come to act wickedly. Still our only chance now was to stand by him; besides his immediate entourage assured us of an explanation. And we remembered how clearly he had been exculpated in the Pigott charges case. As well as I recollect I wrote to Justin McCarthy, and he assured me an explanation would be given. In London, where we went on 24th Nov. I could not see Morley or Justin McCarthy. A fog appeared to envelope everything. We were being cajoled and humbugged and led on to our doom with Machiavellian ingenuity. And at the last on the 25th when the Party met we were led to elect Mr Parnell, supposing that immediately afterwards he would make an explanation or an amende, or perhaps temporarily retire.

Instead of this once trapped into reelecting him, his attitude was that of a heartless rock: not one word of apology or explanation was there to be. And so the eyes of the majority of us were opened. Gladstone's dignified letter was an argument;[154] but in our hearts and consciences without that there was enough to lead us to break with him. His taking up with O'Shea's wife would in itself never have been sufficient reason. It was all the concealment and the lying — the absence of the shade of apology or regret. He was the representative of the honour of Ireland, and he betrayed it for the sake of a worthless woman.

And in his determination to hold his position he broke all bounds of honour and truth; and utterly forfeited our regard.

That some of the best people I know still worship his memory and have his portrait up in every room in their houses is one of the strangest puzzles that have ever presented themselves to my mind; as strange as in subsequent years have been the approval by many people of the Boer War.

The bitterness displayed in the subsequent contest is bitterly to be regretted. Under similar conditions no other people would have been less bitter. We should not have allowed Mr Healy's spirit so to mix with it. And subsequent events have proved that, not patriotism, but personal spite, and a hatred of all placed above him, was the moving spirit with Mr Healy. The cup of hope had been dashed from our lips and we were maddened. That is the best that can be said for us.

Comparisons have sometimes been made with the case of Nelson and Lady Hamilton. The English adore Nelson through all; why should we not adore Parnell? In no case even if an Englishman could I reverence Nelson's memory or place a wreath on his grave. The initial difference between the two cases is this. Nelson was a war hero. Parnell, a political hero. It was Parnell's moral power and influence that was destroyed. But for his action in the O'Shea business and his defence of it, we would have gained Home Rule then. Had Nelson, through his connection with Lady Hamilton lost to England for a generation the empire of the sea, how would the English people regard him and his memory!

In what I have written I may not have been entirely able to explain or justify the position I took up in 1890; and which now, 16 years afterwards, I strongly hold to. My summing up is this. Parnell might have been a second Washington. He sacrificed his country to his selfishness and pride as did Napoleon.

Parnell had great qualities and played a great and useful part up to the moment of his fall. He broke his life. It was not rounded off and perfected as was the life of him whose remains we have just laid in the earth at Strade.

Alfred Webb
4th June 1906

Abbreviations

DNB	*Dictionary of National Biography*
FHL	Friends' Historical Library, Dublin
NLI	National Library of Ireland, Dublin
TCD	Trinity College, Dublin

Notes to Introduction

1   M. V. Kamath, 'The Men and Women who Fought for Freedom', *The Leela* (Independence Day issue), ii (2 Aug.–Sept. 1997), p. 3.

2   This section on the Webb family is drawn from Richard S. Harrison, *Richard Davis Webb: Dublin Quaker Printer (1805–72)* (Skibbereen, 1993).

3   The correspondence of Richard Davis Webb with the anti-slavery movement is in the Boston Public Library.

4   Harrison, *Webb*, p. 2.

5   Ibid., pp. 47–8.

6   In 1857 Alfred Webb told the Dublin Monthly Meeting that he felt he did not 'act as would become a consistent member of any religious persuasion': Harrison, *Webb*, p. 78 n. 100; minute in the case of Alfred Webb, 2 mo. [Feb.], 1858: FHL, PORT 64, folder 1.2h.

7   Obituary of Alfred Webb, *Freeman's Journal*, 1 Aug. 1908; Webb, Autobiography, ff. 116–17, 120–22: FHL.

8   *DNB* entry for Webb.

9   Deborah Webb, 'Reminiscences', *Freeman's Journal*, 3 Aug. 1908.

10   Elizabeth (Lizzie) Shackleton (1834–1907) was the sixth child of George Shackleton of Ballitore and his wife Hannah Fisher.

11   *Thom's Directory*, 1850.

12   Webb, Autobiography, ff. 19–23: FHL.

13   Letter to *Argus*, 24 July 1854. (Cuttings of the newspaper items cited throughout the Introduction are contained in NLI, MS 1745.)

14   Letter to *Freeman's Journal*, 12 Apr. [year unknown, cutting in NLI, MS 1745]; notice, ibid., 24 June 1880.

15   Letter to *New Ireland*, 24 May 1870.

16   Webb, Autobiography, ff. 395–6: FHL; leaflet, 5 July 1884: NLI, MS 1745.

17   Letter to *Daily News*, 1 Dec. 1866.

18   Motion put by Webb to the Irish Antiquarian and Historical Association: NLI, MS 1745, f. 82.

19 *Daily News*, 1 Dec. 1866. Lecky wrote of the 'ceaseless ridicule, the unwavering contempt, the studied depreciation of the Irish character and intellect habitual in the English newspapers' in the first edition of his *Leaders of Public Opinion in Ireland* (London, 1861), pp. 302–3.

20 Letter 'to an enquiring friend in England', *Manchester Examiner*, 20 Feb. 1866.

21 Webb, Autobiography, f. 406.

22 Letter to *Manchester Examiner*, 20 Feb. 1866.

23 In his text Webb has reversed the chronological order of these events (see p. 38).

24 Joseph Spence, 'Isaac Butt, Nationality and Irish Toryism, 1833–1852', *Bullán*, ii (1995), p. 57.

25 David Thornley, *Isaac Butt and Home Rule* (London, 1964), p. 96.

26 Webb to Daunt, 12 Apr. 1871, quoted in Thornley, *Butt*, p. 139.

27 Thornley, *Butt*, p. 162.

28 *Hansard 3*, cccxlii, 943–4 (14 Mar. 1890).

29 Webb to Parnell, 13 May 1883: NLI, MS 1745, ff. 135–8.

30 The Curtin affair is considered in detail in Rita Morgan, 'A Kerry Moonlighting Tragedy' (M.A. thesis, Birkbeck College, London 1990).

31 Ibid., p. 15.

32 Ibid., p. 7 n. 7; Webb 'To Some of my Nationalist Friends', 27 Jan. 1886: NLI, MS 1745.

33 J. S. Mill, *Principles of Political Economy* (9th ed., 2 vols., London, 1886), i, 408.

34 Mary Cumpston, 'Some Early Indian Nationalists and their Allies in the British Parliament, 1851–1906', *English Historical Review*, lxxvi (1961), pp. 281–2. I am grateful to Patrick Gill for drawing my attention to this article.

35 In 1897 Gokhale told Dillon that he had followed the events in Ireland with 'deep, almost passionate' interest for the previous ten years. Webb to Dillon, 5 June 1897; Gokhale to Dillon, 24 June 1897: TCD, Dillon Papers, MS 6760/1700.

36 Dadabhai Naoroji (1825–1917), one of the founders of the Indian National Congress, and the first Indian elected to the House of Commons. He became MP for Central Finsbury in 1892. See *DNB* entry; Michael Davitt, *The Fall of Feudalism in Ireland; or The Story of the Land League Revolution* (London, 1904), p. 447.

37 R. P. Masani, *Dadabhai Naoroji: the Grand Old Man of India* (London, 1939), pp. 236, 335–6.

38 Ibid., p. 238. 'There is no fear that you will excite a rebellion in India if you are elected by an Irish constituency to an Irish seat in the heart of a rebellious locality': Wacha to Naoroji, 10 July 1888: *Correspondence of Dadabhai Naoroji*, ed. R. P. Patwardhan (2 vols, New Delhi, 1977), ii, pt 1, p. 101.

39 'England's Imperial Despotism: Indian Portents', *Weekly Freeman*, 17 July 1897.

40 Sir Dinsha Edulji Wacha (1844–1936), manager in the cotton industry in Bombay; studied and wrote on Indian economic problems. One of the first delegates

to the Indian National Congress, he became joint secretary of the Congress and president in 1901. Like Naoroji, he was a Parsee.

41   Robert Spence Watson (1837–1911), a Quaker solicitor and liberal, active in Newcastle-upon-Tyne politics. He wrote on Indian affairs for the *Contemporary Review*.

42   Davitt, *Fall of Feudalism*, p. 549.

43   Wacha to Naoroji,19 Dec. 1894: *Naoroji Correspondence*, ii, pt 1, pp. 418–19.

44   A. M. Zaidi (ed.), *Congress Presidential Addresses*, i: *1885–1900* (New Delhi, 1985), pp. 193–4, 205.

45   Wacha to Naoroji, 5 Jan. 1895: *Naoroji Correspondence*, ii, pt 1, pp. 419–20.

46   Leaflet : TCD, Dillon Papers, MS 6852/11.

47   Webb to Dillon, 28 Nov. 1892, 20 Aug. 1893: ibid., MS 6760/1659, 1670; Webb to Dillon, 1 July 1895: ibid., MS 6760/1679.

48   Webb to Dillon, 4 Oct. 1893: ibid., MS 6760/1671.

49   Webb to Dillon, 1 Feb. 1894: ibid., MS 6760/1672.

50   Webb to Dillon, 7 Feb. 1897, quoted in Frank Callanan, *T. M. Healy* (Cork, 1996), p. 296 n. 28.

51   P. Poland (Cincinnati) to Dillon, 4 Jan. 1891; J. J. O'Connor to Dillon, 5 Jan. 1891; James Mooney to Dillon, 27 Jan. 1891: TCD, Dillon Papers, MSS 6844/40, 41, 45.

52   Callanan, *Healy*, pp. 448–9; Webb to Dillon, 19 Jan. 1891, 20 Aug. 1893: TCD, Dillon Papers, MSS 6760/1665, 1670.

53   Webb to Dillon, 27 Aug. 1895: TCD, Dillon Papers, MS 6760/1604.

54   Webb to O'Brien, 28 Aug. 1895: NLI, O'Brien Papers, MS 13341 (4).

55   Webb to Dillon, 22 June 1897, 11 Aug. 1900: TCD, Dillon Papers, MSS 6760/1705, 1710.

56   Webb to Dillon 29 Oct. 1903: ibid., MS 6760/1729.

57   Wacha to Naoroji, 5 Jan. 1895: *Naoroji Correspondence*, ii, pt 1, pp. 419–20.

58   Zaidi (ed.), *Congress Presidential Addresses*, i, 198.

59   Callanan, *Healy*, p. 423.

60   Webb to Dillon, 1 Feb. 1894, 17 Aug. 1895: TCD, Dillon Papers, MSS 6760/1672, 1681.

61   T. W. Moody, *Davitt and Irish Revolution, 1846–82* (Oxford, 1981), pp. 549–57.

62   Ibid., pp. 490, 492; Davitt, *Fall of Feudalism*, p. 715.

63   Webb to Dillon, 13 Dec. 1906: TCD, Dillon Papers, MS 6760/1731.

64   Webb to J. N. Rooney, Irish National Federation, 12 June 1897: ibid., MS 6763/131.

65   *Freeman's Journal*,1, 8 Aug. 1908.

Notes to Narrative

1   Richard Webb (1836–82) worked in Richard Davis Webb's printing works and then in the Shackleton flour mills. Spent much of his life in America and Australia. See Pamela Bradley, 'Biographical Index to Alfred Webb, Autobiography' (typescript, 1996): FHL.

2   Deborah Webb (1837–1921), AW's sister. She never married and kept house for her parents and for Alfred Webb in Dublin. See Bradley, 'Biographical Index'.

3   John Mitchel (1815–75), Young Irelander; son of a Presbyterian minister. His *Jail Journal* (New York, 1854), a record of his prison experiences, was an important text for generations of Irish nationalists.

4   Henrietta Martin was on the committee of the Ladies' Land League in 1881. Davitt, *Fall of Feudalism*, p. 457.

5   Asenath Nicholson (1792–1855), American Quaker philanthropist; author of *Ireland's Welcome to the Stranger; or, Excursions through Ireland in 1844 and 1845 for the Purpose of Personally Investigating the Condition of the Poor* (New York, 1847).

6   Percy Bysshe Shelley (1792–1822), poet. Married Harriet Westbrook in 1811. They went to Dublin in February 1812, where he spoke at public meetings and wrote *An Address to the Irish People* and *Proposals for an Association for the Regeneration of Ireland* (both Dublin, 1812). In the following year they returned to Ireland, where their daughter was born.

7   George Downes (*c.* 1790–1846), secretary of the Ballitore Temperance Society. A Norse scholar, he worked on the Ordnance Survey with George Petrie and became assistant librarian of Trinity College, Dublin. See Harrison, *Webb*, p. 13; Bradley, 'Biographical Index'.

8   Edward Dowden (1843–1913), Professor of English Literature, Trinity College, Dublin.

9   Daniel O'Connell (1775–1847), lawyer and politician; organiser and leader of the movement for the repeal of the Act of Union.

10   Richard Dowden (1794–1861), Presbyterian, Cork liberal, and one of the first supporters of Father Mathew; Lord Mayor of Cork four times. See *Journal of the Cork Archaeological and Historical Society*, xxii (1916), pp. 21–4.

11   AW's great-uncle, Jacob Poole of Growtown, Co. Wexford, had three children, Sarah, Elizabeth (Lizzie) and Joseph. R. D. Webb published Jacob Poole's *Glossary of the Forth–Bargy . . . Dialect* (1867). See Bradley, 'Biographical Index'.

12   Theodore Suliot (1800–71) taught classics and French at Ballitore and married Hannah White, a cousin of Alfred Webb's mother, Elizabeth. The family emigrated to America. See Harrison, *Webb*, p. 7; Bradley, 'Biographical Index'.

13   Joshua Jacob (*c.*1805–1877) ran a grocery business in Dublin. He believed that Quakers enjoyed a sybaritic life and that this endangered the health of the Society.

With Abigail Beale of Mountmellick he opened meeting-houses in Dublin, Mountmellick, Waterford and Clonmel in 1840. Their followers, who numbered about forty people, wore white clothing and no shoes. Jacob was eventually arrested for appropriating the possessions of his relatives and was imprisoned for two years for refusing to acknowledge the court or to pay rates and taxes. Believing that he had a divine ordinance to divorce his wife, Jacob was described as having a domineering personality, and as persecuting those who opposed him. He died a member of the Roman Catholic Church. See Isabel Grubb, *Quakers in Ireland* (Dublin, 1929), pp. 127–9.

14 Newenham Harvey (1836–1901), a Waterford printer. See Bradley, 'Biographical Index'.

15 Samuel Vallis Peet (b. 1822), barrister, of 27 Hatch Street, Dublin; born at Waterford and graduated at TCD in 1844. Edward Keane, P. B. Phair and T. U. Sadlier, *King's Inns Admission Papers, 1607–1867* (Dublin, 1982).

16 Robert Chapman (d. 1886) became a partner of R. D. Webb in 1832. Harrison, *Webb*, p. 19.

17 The Statistical Society of Dublin was founded in 1847. William Hancock (1820–88), economist and lawyer, was the moving spirit in its foundation. John Kells Ingram (1823–1907), economist, poet and Vice-Provost of TCD; author of 'The Memory of the Dead' ('Who Fears to Speak of Ninety-Eight?'). Henry Dix Hutton (1825–1907), positivist and correspondent of Comte. Thomas O'Hagan (1822–90), lawyer and politician, defended Charles Gavan Duffy in 1848; in 1868 became the first Catholic Lord Chancellor of Ireland since the imposition of the penal laws. Richard Whately (1787–1863), Protestant Archbishop of Dublin, 1831–63; supported Catholic Emancipation and campaigned for reform of the poor law and education. *Journal of the Statistical Society*, ix (1896), pp. 384–93.

18 Jonathan Pim (1806–85) had been a school friend of Richard Davis Webb at Ballitore. He set up the Central Relief Committee to raise funds and organise relief during the Famine. The committee's report, *Distress in Ireland: Extracts from Correspondence published by the Central Relief Committee of the Society of Friends*, was published in 1847. Pim was MP for Dublin, 1865–74. His *Condition and Prospect of Ireland* was published in 1848. See Harrison, *Webb*, pp. 4, 55; Bradley, 'Biographical Index'.

19 James Haughton (1795–1873), philanthropist, temperance and anti-slavery campaigner. Worked with R. D. Webb in the Hibernian Anti-Slavery Society. See *DNB* entry.

20 Richard Allen (1803–86), a Dublin draper active in the anti-slavery movement. He married Anne Webb in 1828. Richard S. Harrison, *A Biographical Dictionary of Irish Quakers* (Dublin, 1997), p. 25.

21   Charles Gavan Duffy (1816–1903), Young Irelander, journalist and politician.

22   Thomas Cole married Elizabeth Leadbeater (1791–1876), daughter of Mary Leadbeater.

23   The United States declared war on Mexico in 1846 after the failure of negotiations to purchase New Mexico. In the Treaty of Guadalupe Hidalgo, Mexico relinquished large tracts of land which now form five American states. The Fugitive Slave Law, passed in 1851, bound public officials to assist slave-owners to recapture runaway slaves and imposed fines on all those who helped the fugitives. Its severity moved Harriet Beecher Stowe to write *Uncle Tom's Cabin*. Frederick Douglass (1817?–1895), a freed slave, journalist and anti-slavery campaigner, visited Dublin in 1845, where he angered Methodists and Quakers by criticising Methodist slave-holding from a Quaker meeting-house platform. Harrison, *Webb*, p. 119.

24   Dr J. B. Estlin (d. 1855) and Mary Estlin. The *Anti-Slavery Advocate* ran from 1852 to 1863. R. K. Webb, *Harriet Martineau: a Radical Victorian* (London, 1960), pp. 25, 239.

25   Harriet Martineau (1802–76), Unitarian philosopher and economist. R.D. Webb met her after having read her book, *The Martyr Age*, on the evils of slavery. She visited Dublin in 1852. Harrison, *Webb*, p. 23; Webb, *Martineau*, p. 25.

26   Samuel Neilson (1761–1803), United Irishman. See *DNB* entry.

27   John Eustace (1791–1867) founded a mental asylum at Hampstead, near Glasnevin. Joseph Poole, linguist, botanist and artist, was the eldest son of Jacob and Mary Poole of Growtown, Co. Wexford. He was active in the 1848 rebellion, but was never detected. Harrison, *Irish Quakers*, p. 43.

28   The republican organisation founded in 1858 by James Stephens, dedicated to the overthrow by force of British rule in Ireland.

29   William Lloyd Garrison (1805–79), radical American abolitionist and journalist from Boston. R. D. Webb first met him at the world anti-slavery convention held in London in 1840. Like Webb, Garrison held radical views on temperance and women's suffrage. In 1831 he founded *The Liberator*, advocating peaceful resistance to slavery. Harrison, *Webb*, p. 25.

30   Mary Edmondson (1818–1906), daughter of John Wigham of Edinburgh. She was much involved in the temperance movement and the relief of prisoners. Harrison, *Irish Quakers*, p. 42.

31   Wilhelmina Webb, daughter of William Webb and Maria Lamb married a distant relation, 'Red' John Webb. Anna (1833–88), who was involved in a Dublin literary society, 'The Moonlighters', married Abraham Shackleton (1827–1912), a nationalist who became a member of Dublin Corporation. Maria D. Webb (*fl.*1888–1901) painted rustic scenes and married Henry Robinson (*fl.*1884–96). They both exhibited at the Royal Academy, London.

32   Harriet Beecher Stowe (1811–96) was the author of *Uncle Tom's Cabin*, which was
      serialised in the *National Era* in 1851–2 and was published in book form in 1852.

33   Maria Lamb, who married William Webb, was author of *The Fells of Swarthmoor
      Hall* (London, 1865) and *The Penns and Penningtons of the Seventeenth Century*
      (Dublin, 1867). James Webb (1776–1854), AW's grandfather, was the eldest son
      of Joseph Webb and Rebecca Haydock. See Bradley, 'Biographical Index'.

34   Mary Poole (1781–1872), *née* Sparrow, was AW's maternal great-aunt. She expe-
      rienced the 1798 rebellion in Wexford as a child and in later life suffered from
      memories of what had occurred. Jacob Poole (d. 1862) was the son of Jacob and
      Mary Poole of Growtown, Co. Wexford. He was a childhood friend of AW. Mar-
      ried first Hannah Warne of Ballinclay, Co. Wexford, and secondly Hannah Six-
      smith. See Bradley, 'Biographical Index'.

35   Mrs Moore was born a Miss Webb. She married Robert Rowan Ross Moore of
      Manchester. AW and his brother stayed with them when they were at school
      there. See Bradley, 'Biographical Index'.

36   The Encumbered Estates Court, founded under the Encumbered Estates Acts
      1848 and 1849, made possible the sale of mortgaged Irish estates in financial dif-
      ficulty by giving the new owners a clear title to the property.

37   John Thompson married Deborah Webb. They had two children, John and
      William, and lived in Manchester. James Webb, AW's paternal uncle, ran a drap-
      ery shop at Cornmarket, Dublin. He married Anne White. Among their child-
      ren were Joseph (1816–63) and Hannah (1821–77), who was 'Red' John Webb's
      second wife. They lived at De Vesci Lodge, Monkstown. See Bradley, 'Biograph-
      ical Index'.

38   Charlotte Bronte's novel *Jane Eyre* was published in 1847.

39   Anne Allen (1805–68) was a sister of William Webb. She became Richard Allen's
      first wife. See Bradley, 'Biographical Index'.

40   The *United Irishman* was founded by John Mitchel in February 1848 as the mouth-
      piece for his physical-force policy. The paper was suppressed by Dublin Castle in
      May 1848.

41   Perhaps John Webb (1783–1873), a linen draper. Harrison, *Webb*, p. 4.

42   George Petrie (1789–1866), artist and antiquarian; his *Essay on the Round Towers
      of Ireland* was published in 1833. His fellow worker in the Historical Department
      of the Ordnance Survey was John O'Donovan, whose edition of *Annals of the Four
      Masters* was published in seven volumes between 1848 and 1851. The Ordnance
      Survey of Ireland was started in 1830. Its aim was to collect information on local
      topography and economy over the whole country. The Irish Archaeological Soci-
      ety, founded in 1840, was merged with the Celtic Society, founded in 1845 to
      preserve and publish early Irish manuscripts. The Ossianic Society was founded
      in 1853 with the same aim.

43 Webb's *Compendium of Irish Biography* was first published in 1878 and went into a number of editions.

44 Alfred Webb, *Recollections of a Three-Days Tour in the County of Wicklow in the Summer of 1850* [Dublin, c.1856].

45 Henry Joy McCracken (1767–98), United Irishman; tried and hanged in Belfast, 1798. See *DNB* entry.

46 The income from the opium trade from India to China helped Britain to balance its trading account with China. When China banned the import of opium in 1839, Britain used force to maintain it in a series of campaigns which were condemned by liberal opinion at home.

47 A meeting held at the Rotunda, Dublin, on 17 March 1865 resolved to restore and open St Stephen's Green to the public, and to ask the Corporation to levy a ½d rate for its maintenance and improvement. Sir Arthur Guinness donated £5,000 to construct ornamental works. *The Times*, 21 Mar. 1865, 15 June 1876.

48 John McEvoy manufactured soap and candles at 68 Lower George's Street, Kingstown (Dún Laoghaire). M. E. Solomons was 'optician to the Royal Family' at 19 Nassau Street, Dublin. Nugent Robinson was assistant secretary to the Water Works Committee in 1865.

49 In 1861 a proposal to provide Dublin with clean water led to disputes between Dublin Corporation and Rathmines. Sir John Gray, chairman of Dublin Waterworks, successfully negotiated the scheme. *Thom's Directory*, 1865; Mary Daly, *Dublin: the Deposed Capital* (Cork, 1984), p. 228.

50 T. W. Russell (1841–1920), Liberal MP and campaigner for temperance and Sunday closing.

51 Thomas Webb (1806–84), AW's paternal uncle, was a draper in North King Street, Dublin; his son Thomas married Emily Chandlee. See Bradley, 'Biographical Index'.

52 James Alexander Mowatt, manager of the Estates Bank, D'Olier Street, Dublin, edited the *Irish Temperance Star*, which ran from January 1866 to March 1867. See Bradley, 'Biographical Index'; *Thom's Directory*, 1865.

53 Michael Davitt (1846–1906), nationalist politician and early organiser of the Land League. His memoir, *The Fall of Feudalism in Ireland* (London, 1904), is an important record of the Land War.

54 John Brown (1800–59) led a rising in support of abolition at Harper's Ferry, Virginia, in October 1859. He was tried and sentenced to death. Although R. D. Webb and his friends supported the cause of abolition, they were deeply concerned about the use of violence in its support. Harrison, *Webb*, p. 71.

55 'Obstruction' was a filibustering tactic adopted by members of the Irish Parliamentary Party in 1877, and principally promoted by Joseph Gillis Biggar (1828–90) and C. S. Parnell, to delay the passage of important English and Scottish legislation.

56   George Addey, a Cork draper, married Elizabeth (1818–86), daughter of Jacob
      and Mary Poole of Growtown, Co. Wexford.

57   On 5 March 1867 a Fenian rising in seven counties failed and a large number of
      Fenians were arrested. Later that year the government commissioned an inquiry
      into the treatment of Fenian prisoners. See Bradley, 'Biographical Index'; *The
      Times*, 8 Mar. 1867.

58   John O'Leary (1830–1907), President of the Supreme Council of the Irish
      Republican Brotherhood, 1885–1907. Thomas Clarke Luby (1822–1901),
      nationalist and early supporter of James Stephens. Charles Joseph Kickham
      (1828–82), Fenian and writer.

59   William Keogh (1817–78), politician and judge, an early supporter of tenant
      right, he incurred the undying wrath of nationalists for accepting the post of Solic-
      itor General; committed suicide.

60   AW refers to Gladstone's coercion legislation which, like many others, he
      regarded as being at odds with the younger Gladstone's views on prisons in
      Naples, exemplified in his letters to Lord Aberdeen (1851), in which he had
      described Bourbon rule in Italy as 'the negation of God erected into a system of
      government'.

61   Ellen O'Leary (1831–89), writer and republican.

62   William Allen, Michael Larkin and Michael O'Brien were part of a group of five
      Fenians who attempted to rescue two of their captured leaders in Manchester in
      1867, during which a policeman was killed. At their trial considerable doubt was
      cast on the reliability of the evidence against them, and two men were released.
      The public execution of Allen, Larkin and O'Brien, and the subsequent com-
      memorative demonstration in Dublin, mobilised Irish public opinion against the
      British government, and the three became known as the 'Manchester Martyrs'.

63   The Amnesty campaign was founded in 1868 to campaign for the release of
      imprisoned members of the Irish Republican Brotherhood. Its president was Isaac
      Butt.

64   Alexander Martin Sullivan (1830–84), journalist and politician; proprietor and
      editor of *The Nation*. Timothy Daniel Sullivan (1827–1914), journalist and politi-
      cian, author of 'God Save Ireland'; prosecuted with Parnell in 1880; Lord Mayor
      of Dublin, 1886–87.

65   Richard Pigott (1828–89), journalist. His newspaper concerns were purchased
      by the Irish Parliamentary Party. He forged documents with Charles Stewart Par-
      nell's signature, was exposed during the Special Commission hearings in 1889,
      fled the country, and committed suicide in a Madrid hotel.

66   Captain John Dunne was a close associate and longstanding friend of Isaac Butt.
      He served as secretary of the Home Government Association. Thornley, *Butt*, pp.
      93, 105.

67 Donal Sullivan (1838–1907), MP for South Westmeath, 1885–1907; secretary of the Irish Parliamentary Party, 1893–98.

68 William Martin Murphy (1844–1919), politician and newspaper proprietor. T. M. Healy (1855–1931), nationalist politician and writer; served as Parnell's secretary, but broke with Parnell in 1886 over the latter's relationship with Katharine O'Shea.

69 Possibly John Barnes, lawyer, of 69 St Stephen's Green, Dublin. See *Thom's Directory*, 1865.

70 Daniel O'Donoghue (1833–89), Whig politician; MP for Tralee, 1865–85; supporter of Parnell. Isaac Butt (1813–79), Protestant lawyer and nationalist politician; chairman of Home Rule Party, 1874–79.

71 The Home Government Association was inaugurated by Isaac Butt in 1870. It aimed to establish a federal system of government for the United Kingdom and give Ireland a parliament empowered to decide on internal affairs. It remained active until 1873, when it was succeeded by the Home Rule League.

72 Richard Davis Webb died in 1872.

73 The Home Government Association held a conference at the Rotunda, Dublin, 18–21 November 1873, when it was reconstituted as the Irish Home Rule League, whose policy was to obtain self-government.

74 John Gordon Swift MacNeill (1849–1926), nationalist politician and constitutional lawyer; MP for South Donegal, 1887–1918.

75 Probably that by John Butler Yeats.

76 Alexander Pope, *Essay on Man* (London, 1711), l. 281.

77 Rev. Joseph A. Galbraith (1818–90) was elected Erasmus Smith Professor of Natural and Experimental Philosophy at TCD in 1854; resigned from his professorship in 1868. John Martin (1812–75), Liberal MP for Meath, 1871–75; secretary of the Amnesty Committee in 1869. See *Dublin University Calendars*; Moody, *Davitt*, p. 178; Thornley, *Butt*, p. 67.

78 Mitchell Henry (1826–1910), nationalist politician; MP for Co. Galway, 1871–85. A wealthy landowner, he worked for Home Rule but dissented from the policies of the Land League.

79 Sir John Pentland Mahaffy (1839–1919), first Professor of Ancient History, Trinity College, Dublin,1869; Provost, 1914–19.

80 John Francis Maguire (1815–72), newspaper proprietor and politician; supporter of Daniel O'Connell and founder of the *Cork Examiner*.

81 Rev. Theobald Mathew(1790–1856), O.F.M.Cap., abolitionist and temperance reformer.

82 John Blunden was a secretary of the Home Rule League. Thornley, *Butt*, p. 247.

83 P. J. Smyth (1823–85), Young Irelander and Home Rule politician. He later rejected physical-force politics and was opposed to the Land League.

84 John Dillon (1851–1927), land campaigner and nationalist politician. Opposed Parnell in the split in the Irish Parliamentary Party and led the anti-Parnellites after 1896. With John Redmond, he reunited the Irish Parliamentary Party in 1900.

85 William Joseph O'Neill Daunt (1807–94), Home Rule politician and writer; secretary of the Home Government Association.

86 Dr Richard Grattan, author of *Considerations on the Human Mind, its Present State, and Future Destination* (London, 1861). A descendant of Henry Grattan, he was an eccentric thorn in the side of the Home Government Association. Co-founder, with John Eustace, of the Hampstead Asylum at Glasnevin. Thornley, *Butt*, p. 108.

87 John MacHale (1791–1881), Catholic Archbishop of Tuam. A supporter of Repeal, he worked to bring the attention of the British government to the consequences of the Famine in the west of Ireland. Although he had supported tenant right, he condemned the formation of the Land League in Connacht.

88 Dr Robert Dyer Lyons (1826–86), physician and liberal politician who favoured the creation of a state-funded Irish peasant proprietary.

89 Sir John Gray (1816–75), journalist and Repeal politician; advanced Liberal MP for Kilkenny, 1865–75; proprietor of the *Freeman's Journal*.

90 Charles Stewart Parnell (1846–91), politician; chairman of the Irish Parliamentary Party, 1880–90.

91 The Irish National Land League was formed in October 1879 with C. S. Parnell as President. Its object was to protect tenants and fight landlordism.

92 A conference convened in Dublin by Michael Davitt which met at the Rotunda on 29 April 1880. It endorsed the policies of the Land League and committed Parnellite MPs to its programme.

93 Richard Whately, *Historic Doubts relative to Napoleon Buonaparte* (London, 1819).

94 Dr Joseph Edward Kenny (1845–1900), surgeon and Parnellite politician. William Hoey Kearney Redmond (1861–1917), politician and brother of John Redmond; helped to establish the United Irish League in the United States. Andrew Kettle (1833–1916), persuaded Parnell to support the land agitation in the 1870s; advocated that the Irish Party should leave Westminster and campaign in Ireland; imprisoned for involvement in coercion.

95 Lord Frederick Cavendish (1836–82), Liberal politician, became Chief Secretary for Ireland in May 1882. He was murdered with T. H. Burke (1829–82), Under-Secretary for Ireland, in Phoenix Park, immediately after he had arrived in Ireland. Responsibility for the assassination was first put on Parnell's supporters, but it was in fact carried out by the Invincibles, a Fenian splinter group.

96 James Carey (1845–83), a member of the Invincibles, and involved in the Phoenix Park murders. He subsequently became an informer, and his evidence led to the conviction of five of his accomplices. He was later murdered.

97 Webb was member of Dublin Corporation and the Port and Harbour Board from

1882 to 1883. The Lord Mayor of Dublin referred to was either Charles Dawson, 1882–3, or William Meagher, 1884.

98   An exhibition of Irish Arts and Manufactures was held in the Rotunda Hospital gardens in Dublin in August 1882.

99   The Irish National League replaced the Land League in October 1882 as the policy-making body of the Irish Parliamentary Party. It had branches throughout Ireland organised from Dublin and provided financial support for impecunious Irish MPs. The League split when the Irish Parliamentary Party divided in 1890 over Parnell's relationship with Mrs O'Shea.

100   The Central Land League of the Ladies of Ireland was founded in 1881 with the support of Michael Davitt and was headed by Anna Parnell. Its members collected information on conditions on estates throughout Ireland, and when Parnell and other leaders were imprisoned the Ladies' Land League organised the movement and published the Land League newspaper, *United Ireland*. Parnell disliked the Ladies' Land League and brought the organisation to an end in 1882. Moody, *Davitt*, pp. 456–7; Anna Parnell, *The Tale of a Great Sham*, ed. Dana Hearne (Dublin, 1986).

101   Hannah Lynch was the daughter of a Fenian and was brought up in a political and literary household and educated in France. When *United Ireland* was shut down in October 1881, she took the type to France and arranged for it to be printed there. Katherine Tynan Hinkson (1861–1931), one of the founders of the Ladies' Land League, is best known as a poet and novelist who became closely associated with W. B. Yeats and the Gaelic revival.

102   Anna Catherine Parnell (1852–1911), agitator and sister of C. S. Parnell. Worked on famine relief in the 1870s. She thought the Land League policies weak and founded the more radical Ladies' Land League with her sister Frances (Fanny). Estranged from her brother when he refused to fund her organisation, she moved to England and died in a drowning accident.

103   The United Irish League was founded by William O'Brien in 1898 at Westport, Co. Mayo, to draw attention to the agricultural depression in the west. Under the slogan 'The Land for the People', it campaigned for the redistribution of large estates to small farmers, and it attacked land-grabbers.

104   Mark Anthony McDonnell (1854–1906), surgeon and nationalist politician; MP for Leix, 1892–1906.

105   John Campbell Gordon (1847–1934), 1st Marquis of Aberdeen and Temair (1847–1934), liberal politician; Lord Lieutenant of Ireland 1886, 1905–15. His wife Ishbel was active in Irish health welfare schemes.

106   Col. Alfred Turner succeeded Redvers Buller as Commissioner for Kerry and Clare and implemented Balfour's coercion legislation.

107   Arthur James Balfour, Chief Secretary, 1887–91, brought in the Criminal Law

Amendment Act, 1887, which gave powers to proclaim districts considered to be
dangerous.

108 Elizabeth Dunn was an Irishwoman born in England who became a close friend
of AW's sister Deborah.

109 Sir Arthur Edward Guinness, Bart (1840–1915), Unionist politician; MP for
Dublin City, 1874–80; created Baron Ardilaun, 1880.

110 John Morley (1838–1923), later 1st Viscount Morley of Blackburn, journalist
and Liberal politician; Chief Secretary for Ireland, 1886, 1892–95. James Bryce
(1838–1922), Liberal politician; Chief Secretary for Ireland, 1905–7. William
Morris (1834–96), writer, artist, manufacturer and socialist. George John Shaw
Lefevre (1831–1928), 1st Baron Eversley, Liberal MP, 1864–95; interested in
Irish agrarian reform.

111 Edmund Dwyer Gray (1845–88), journalist and nationalist politician, son of Sir
John Gray; supporter of Parnell.

112 Valentine Blake Dillon, Lord Mayor of Dublin, 1894–95.

113 Wilfrid Scawen Blunt (1840–1922), English writer and diplomat, supported the
Irish Parliamentary Party and was imprisoned in 1887 for advocating the Plan of
Campaign. He married Lady Anne Noel, grand-daughter of Lord Byron and Ada
Lovelace.

114 Henry Norman (1858–1939), journalist and traveller, wrote on Russia and Japan,
and on the Bodyke evictions.

115 Norma Borthwick illustrated *The Irish Alphabet* (Dublin, 1900) and compiled *Irish
Reading Lessons* (Dublin, 1902), illustrated by Jack B. Yeats. She also translated
Hans Andersen into Irish.

116 Rose Kavanagh (1859–91), poet and friend of John O'Leary. She published
poems and stories in the *Irish Fireside*.

117 William Archibald Macdonald (b. 1841), blind Parnellite MP for Ossory division,
1886–92. See M. Stenton, *Who's Who of British Members of Parliament* (Hassocks,
1976), ii. 231.

118 Henry George (1839–97), American political economist and land reformer who
advocated the Marxist theory of surplus value. George visited Ireland in 1881 and
lectured on the land question, advocating that landlords should pay tax on their
rents; this would redress injustice and also make other taxation unnecessary. He
was barred from re-entering Ireland, but returned in 1884.

119 Charlotte Grace O'Brien (1845–1909), poet and campaigner for the relief of
emigrants. Her reports of conditions on emigrant ships led to the imposition of
stricter government control.

120 Alexander Thom & Co., publishers of official documents and directories.

121 Frances Anna Maria, Countess Russell (1815–98), widow of Lord John Russell,
Prime Minister, 1846–52, 1865–66.

122 Patrick Joseph Power (1850–1913), nationalist politician; MP for East Waterford, 1885–1913.

123 William O'Brien (1852–1928), nationalist politician, agitator and journalist. Edited Parnell's newspaper, *United Ireland*, from 1881 to 1890. Leader of the Plan of Campaign. Became an anti-Parnellite after the split in the Irish Parliamentary Party in 1890. Withdrew from parliamentary politics and campaigned for the relief of distress in the west of Ireland. Founded the United Irish League in 1898. O'Brien married Sophie Raffalovich, the daughter of a wealthy Russian financier, in June 1890.

124 James Patrick O'Gorman Mahon (the O'Gorman Mahon) (1800–91), politician. Supporter of Daniel O'Connell. Travelled widely and returned to Ireland in 1871. Supported Parnell until the split.

125 Sir Thomas Henry Grattan Esmonde, Bart (1862–1935), nationalist politician; MP for South Co. Dublin, 1885–92, West Kerry, 1891–1900, and North Wexford, 1900–18. Edmund Francis Vesey Knox (1865–1921), a barrister; MP for Londonderry City, 1895–99.

126 William O'Shea (1840–1905), Home Rule politician. Married Katharine Wood in 1867. Used his wife's relationship with Parnell to further his career. Ignored her affair with Parnell until 1889, when he sued for divorce. The case destroyed Parnell's reputation.

127 Justin McCarthy (1830–1912), politician and writer; leader of the anti-Parnellites in the Irish Parliamentary Party after the split in 1890; chairman of their constituency organisation, the Irish National Federation.

128 Richard Barry O'Brien (1847–1918), historian. Remained loyal to Parnell after the split in 1890 and wrote his biography.

129 William Ewart Gladstone (1809–98), Liberal politician, four times Prime Minister, who tried and failed to achieve Home Rule for Ireland.

130 Charles Bradlaugh (1833–91), Radical politician.

131 Henry Labouchere (1831–1912), journalist and advanced Liberal politician who supported Home Rule.

132 Sir Wilfred Lawson (1829–1906), Radical politician and supporter of Home Rule.

133 Dr Katherine Bushnell and Elizabeth Andrew, American missionaries with the World Women's Christian Temperance Union, who investigated military prostitution in India in 1891–92. Philippa Levine, 'Venereal Disease, Prostitution, and the Politics of Empre: The Case of British India', *Journal of the History of Sexuality*, iv (1994), pp. 600–1.

134 The *Port Yarrock* sank off Tralee Bay on 28 January 1894 with the loss of twenty-five lives. An inquiry found the owner, Robert Rowat, guilty of sailing short-handed and failing to instruct the master to send for assistance. Rowat was never

prosecuted because of insufficient evidence. *The Times* 30 Jan. 1894, 13 Mar. 1895.

135 Rt Hon. Charles Schwann (1844–1929), advanced Liberal politician who spoke on Indian affairs. Changed his name to Swann in 1913.

136 Sarah Anne Cooke married David Duncan, a Manchester Quaker. She frequently visited Ireland. Their daughter Elizabeth married Charles Schwann.

137 John Francis Xavier O'Brien (1828–1905), nationalist politician and republican. Joined the Fenians in the United States. Took part in the rising of 1867, tried, sentenced to death, and released in 1869. MP for South Mayo, 1885–95, and Cork City, 1895–1905. Became an anti-Parnellite after the split in 1890.

138 Mary A. M. Hoppus, wife of Alfred Marks, was a prolific novelist who also wrote tracts on the Corn Laws, the American War of Independence and land law in England.

139 Lady Agatha Russell (1853–1933), daughter of Lord John Russell, the former Prime Minister (see note 121); a supporter of Home Rule.

140 Thomas Moore (1779–1852), writer and composer. Best known for his *Melodies*, which went into many editions.

141 Margaret Emily Shore's memoir, *Journal of Emily Shore* (London, 1891), is a record of domestic life and natural history.

142 Hannah E. White (1820–97) was a daughter of John and Sally White.

143 'Anna Liffey' was Abraham Shackleton's house at Lucan, where his mills were situated.

144 Mary Hayden was a member of the National Literary Society in 1892, when W. B. Yeats was honorary secretary. *The Collected Letters of W. B. Yeats*, ed. John Kelly, i: *1865–95* (Oxford, 1981), p. 312n.

145 Alexander Ireland (1810–94), journalist.

146 John Francis Waller (1809–94), poet, lawyer and founder member and editor of the *Dublin University Magazine*.

147 The interrupter was a Miss Muller. She insisted on putting an amendment to a resolution on the abolition of the Secretary of State's Council, was ruled out of order by Webb and told by delegates to sit down. Wacha to Naoroji, 5 Jan. 1895: *Naoroji Correspondence*, ii, pt 1, p. 419.

148 Jamsetji Nusserwanji Tata (1861–1904), wealthy Parsee industrialist and developer of Bombay; supporter of the Indian National Congress.

149 George Robert Canning (1815–1932), 4th Baron Harris, Governor of Bombay, 1890–95.

150 Sir William Wilson Hunter (1840–1900), Indian civil servant; author of a large number of works on the history and statistics of India.

151 G. W. E. Russell (1853–1919), Radical MP and social reformer; Under-Secretary of State for India, 1892.

152 John Morley, *The Life of William Ewart Gladstone* (London, 1903).
153 Michael Davitt was buried on 2 June 1906 at Straide, Co. Mayo.
154 On 24 November 1890 Gladstone wrote a letter to John Morley which was intended to be shown to Parnell before the meeting of the Irish Parliamentary Party. The letter expressed Gladstone's view that, notwithstanding the services rendered by Parnell to Ireland, he should resign his leadership of the party.

Bibliography

Bradley, Pamela, 'Biographical Index to Alfred Webb, Autobiography' (typescript, 1996: Friends' Historical Library, Dublin)

Callanan, Frank, *T. M. Healy* (Cork, 1996)

Cumpston, Mary, 'Some Early Indian Nationalists and their Allies in the British Parliament, 1851–1906', *English Historical Review*, lxxvi (1961) pp. 279–97

Daly, Mary, *Dublin: the Deposed Capital* (Cork, 1984)

Grubb, Isabel, *Quakers in Ireland* (Dublin, 1929)

Harris, F. R., *Jamsetji Nusserwanji Tata* (London, 1925)

Harrison, Richard S., *Richard Davis Webb: Dublin Quaker Printer (1805–72)* (Skibbereen, 1993)

—- 'Irish Quaker Perspectives on the Anti-Slavery Movement', *Journal of the Friends' Historical Society*, lvi (1990–93), pp. 106–25

—- *A Biographical Dictionary of Irish Quakers* (Dublin, 1996)

Hinkson, Katherine Tynan, *Twenty-Five Years: Reminiscences* (London, 1913)

Levine, Philippa, 'Venereal Disease, Prostitution, and the Politics of Empire: The Case of British India', *Journal of the History of Sexuality*, iv (1994), pp. 579–602

Masani, R. P., *Dadabhai Naoroji: the Grand Old Man of India* (London, 1939)

Moody, T. W., *Davitt and Irish Revolution, 1846–82* (Oxford, 1981)

Parnell, Anna, *The Tale of a Great Sham*, ed. Dana Hearne (Dublin, 1986)

Naoroji, Dadabhai, *Correspondence*, ed. R. P. Patwardhan, (2 vols, New Delhi, 1977)

Thornley, David, *Isaac Butt and Home Rule* (London, 1964)

Webb, R. K., *Harriet Martineau: a Radical Victorian* (London, 1960)

Yeats, W. B., *Collected Letters*, i: *1865–1895*, ed. John Kelly (Oxford, 1986)

Zaidi, A. M. (ed.), *Congress Presidential Addresses:*, i: *1885–1900* (New Delhi, 1985)

Index